Win Lose Live And Sometimes Opinions

James Greene

Published by James Greene, 2020.

WIN LOSE LIVE AND SOMETIMES OPINIONS

First edition. October 2, 2020.

Copyright © 2020 James Greene.

ISBN: 978-1393850090

Written by James Greene.

Also by James Greene

Thanks again to Self-Publishing Services for the edits.

To mentors, whose hands that are hopefully unbitten.

1

Win

Lose

Opinion?

"I'm right!"

"You're wrong!" "You don't know what you are talking about!"
"I don't care!" "You're misinformed!" "You've lost me!"
"Don't tell me what to do!" "You're crazy!"
If I catch that A—hole! "Quit being so mean!" "That's funny!"
"I like you" "Be careful." "He's forcing my hand."
"You're going to be fun to mess with!" "That's stupid!" "Hold on!"
"She did it!"

"Quit interrupting me!" "They're ignorant!" "Keep your mouth shut!"

"Shut up!" "Let me finish!" "I win!" "You lost!"

"Just listen to me for a moment!" "They need to quit running their mouth"

"Be happy!" "Go f—k yourself!"

"I beat you!" "I got you!" "You're mine!" "I totally owned him with that one!"

Possession? Opinion? Competition? Obsession?

How did we get here?

Socrates lives among us and his *daemon* speaks. Would these be the voices in his head?[1]

There's more going on than a highly competitive nature infesting every part of our societal characterizations. Activities are no longer geared towards expressive discussion with one another, are they? We've entered into a gaming scenario—to win, out duel, and out wit—where saying more or getting in the last word is equated with the last one standing.

Philosopher Georg Simmel called it "antagonistic games," or *kampfspiel*.[2] This was an internal and mental conquest, or mind games if you wish to call it so. This kind of gaming did indeed have sociological components to it. "At any rate, in its *sociological motivation,* the antagonistic game contains is absolutely nothing but the fight itself."[3] Simmel noted that these games are not set up for the attainment of a prize other than simply mastery over the adversary or opponent.

Does every thought, discussion, and activity eventually become the itemization between victors and the defeated? There are other options: Simply be entertained or do nothing about it. Take it. Stand up for yourself. Get thick-skinned. You could prepare for battle and begin to barrage, argue, argue, and argue some more! Or, perhaps, in a passive or docile way, give off a bit of appeasement, knowing that deep down you don't care or don't even wish to entertain the values of winning and losing.

Because of this "game" we can't be certain that any opinion is intended to bring us closer to any facts, stances worth standing with, or realization of any kind. It's all rather overtly obsessive and possessive. Become active to render docile. The opinion must hold sway upon someone, as object. It is juxtaposed positioning to be found out, used, bartered, controlled, banned, marketed, or obligated. "He said this," or "so-and-so said it is this and did this to me," and "I don't like that." She's wrong." "That's not right."

Maybe there's something worth giving a fundamental question to: Is any of this really a language at all?

Philosopher Emmanuel Levinas once exclaimed that truth must result "from its subject in the world and history through labor, cultural creation, and political organization,"[4] something so indicative and clearly observed through our languages with one another. Language is either a confession of truth or disclosure of being.[5]

Now, however, it seems this may not be the case. We are commanded and we command one another with remarks, quips, and jabs. This could be symptomatic of something.

Several years ago Alexandre Kojève implied that the "end of history," as he so declared it, would issue forth symptoms of its arrival. For example, the post-historical realm consists of an animality where our language is reduced to banter, calling, haranguing, or buzzing. The antagonistic game play—to fight just for the reward of the fight—may actually assist in the disappearance of human language for its animalistic formations. This dissipation of the human capacity to confess truth or render word with being becomes likened to a "substitution by mimetic or sonic signals comparable to the language of bees."[6]

It also appears difficult to relegate opinions to a method of interpretation at the moment. The opinion no longer assists us in opening up truth, nor lighting up perspective, worldview, vision, angles, or nuances. Opinions were once part and parcel to understanding, a key component in deriving truth or discovering the matter at hand. In its oldest primordial form is the opening event, the gates of possibility, the procedure of bringing sight by the sounds of rhetoric, speech, and its recognition.

As such in our current conception the opinion holds itself so right and immovable that it wishes to freeze time as if it is a statue of an old god waiting at the gates, tactically guarding against opposition. The person says what they think, all the while ready for self-defense. "That's what I think. Now leave me alone" is what they really mean. Better yet, "That's what I think," actually means, "Do you want to argue? Do you want to fight about it?" "This is my opinion" translates as "I'm right and you're wrong." The opinion is won by force. It's won and considered right if the fight is won. We begin to takes sides to be inherently conflicting and, at the same time, incited and exploited, thereby fueling this gaming notion. As informational access the game gathers its intelligence: "this is so-and-so's opinion on this," or "she said this about such-and-such," and so forth. In other words, "now we have dirt, some juicy gossip, leverage, or a bartering chip." Everyday interaction with opinion and others is part and parcel to a game like, competitive atmosphere, but this is not all.

Opinions are no longer seen as artifice or emotive expression from living, sentient, free beings. Now opinions are something to be categorized, jostled, ordered, opposed, measured, or avoided. The contenders of this game tactically wait for thought and utterance in order to respond with a back-hand by a racquet upon a tennis ball. They wish to get a one-up, to get points toward victory. If my opinion wins the game, if I beat them by tactically using "my" interaction with "their" opinion, then my opinion is right. If I have more people, more references, or just more stuff that represents my opinion, then I win.

We unknowingly even compete in daily conversation, often taken for granted.

Someone may say that they went to such-and-such place, and someone else may respond with "Yeah I've been there. I did that," and in the competitive spirit they one-up with, "I went here. Did you try that? You didn't? Well, when I was there we did this and that and this."

More. More. More. Gaining. Quantifying. Better. Beat 'em. Got 'em. I win.

The opinion is status.

The opinion normalizes.

It names the individual who wishes to individuate. It identifies person or group—me versus not-me. It situates against person or group by strategy. "Oh, I heard so-and so-said such-and-such." "Don't worry. We will get 'em. They can't act that way toward us. I'll make sure of it."

Even daily happenstances may be suspect. Artistic displays, interpretive quests for meaning, or even a technique that opens opinionated emergences with each other—none of these are important anymore. Rather, these are tactics and rigorous techniques derived from authoritative practices to discover a name to call, beckon, harness, and modify the other.

It goes by the procedures of "He is crazy," "She is this" "He is that," "Did you know so-and-so believes such-and-such?" "I think you are this!" "You should do this," and so on. It goes by the assessment of ability: "They didn't do this." "I can't do that." "She must do." "Did they do?" Opinions are reduced to the aspect of "do," "should," "don't," "be," "go," "get away," "be gone." They are reduced into concepts like ban, own, thwart, deflect, avoid, win, and conquer.

If our language is supposed to either confess truth or disclose being, then it is done so in a peculiar way. The "this" or "that" is the name that positions the pieces in a competitive system of ordering. It becomes an arena for sporting and playing upon the other, to get the individual to disclose means that one must use to leverage an opening or fissure and bring about a confession or catharsis while all participators may be laid subject to a potential hastily generalizable procedure altogether. Authority simply makes up reasons. It has to by necessity. It's cloaked and covered. Reason is masked by rationalization. It gets around your opinion or uses it as a tool or means. It doesn't care.

There is an "opinion" of it." Remarks permeate the fields of experiences such as "he is this," "she did this," an "it," this object kind of "thing" that we are made to be. The object of a "that" simply expressed to us as "that" is what it is. It is what it is? The human as object, the invariable and imaginative substitutions, qualities, characterization, and categorizations are applied. There is an indifference we wish to apply to the object. Objectivity expresses indifference.[7]

The object objects.

The opponent or adversary in deeds or rhetoric becomes the object that stands before us as an obstacle or "thing." "It" must be commanded. Move it. Push it around, place it, position it, leverage, trap, design, chip away at it, scurry it along to our will—force and violence. The person, the human animal itself becomes this indifference that signifies to consciousness "the order which, through consciousness shows itself—being would, precisely, impugn."[8]

This is quite possibly a failure of modern thinking. The ancient Greeks for example "could barely even speak of a *thing.*"[9] Yes, the ancients did have a kind of "praxis" for living, and yet quite the contrasting and contentious nature about it also.[10] Hans-Georg Gadamer once noted that the modern modes of force, dissension, and opposition happen distinctly as an abrupt disturbance and insurrection seen, described, and felt within a corporality that must be mastered. In other words, there are modern tools such as the instrument, science, and beyond. We need this "object" of our thoughts, *gegenständ,*[11] something standing against us, or "that which stands over us or opposed to us as something to be overcome."[12] Culminating into a "this" or "that," the object exudes the very clues and reasons behind it. Gadamer was adamantly aware of the problem in his own vernacular *gegenständ* was an object standing, or a stance position. Yet he also evoked the foreign word we know as "object" (*objekt*) and "objectivity"(*objektivität*). The modern design of these concepts "in which human beings seek to make themselves at home in the world"[13] is at issue.

The opinion is the catalyst for the pure energy of emotional exchange and fervor. Opinion is also the object of entanglement. Opinion, knowingly or not, becomes part of "proto cultural packets,"[14] both energetic and containable, and therefore packaged, marketed, and distributed. Opinion is the fuel in the reserve, lying dormant and waiting for access. The emotional effervescence and exchange frequencies of emotional affect proceed to impact, push, and pull self and other. So very often are tethering tensions that become tactics to derive force or marginally dupe someone, thereby gauging, gaining, or ascertaining an emotional reaction. This could be for sheer entertainment value, to make one feel better, to observe the display as if it were a show, or simply to control.

The "antagonistic game" holds a kind of mental and spiritual component. Life begins to emanate into newly generalized schema, a contradiction in form—such is dualism and opposition.[15] The generalized formation is the antithesis to life's emanation and vibrancy. A generalized schema therefore overpowers its uniqueness.[16]

Regardless, if merely described as "antagonistic games," they indeed trend enormously. Simmel once noted how antagonism is hardly ever absent from its sociological elements. It will not be difficult to describe how antagonism leads into something economic, historical, philosophic and beyond either. "One *unites* in order to fight, and one fights under the mutually recognized control of names and rules."[17] And so the purpose and outcome of this game play is to fight? All that's left, it seems, are the objects and commands of these battles, and the groups that swarm among them. This sets up an invariable array of substitutions—what Simmel described as life's opposition against forms. To allude to and foreshadow these writings presented before you, even Simmel himself had a remarkable realization. He went so far as to describe how these "games" enter a "complete dualism," and indeed "presuppose sociological forms in the stricter sense of the word, namely, unification."[18] This antagonism—the corporeal standing of object that incites us—makes us indifferent by invariably substituting, commanding, and willing each other about "its role can increase to infinity, that is, to the point of suppressing all convergent elements."[19]

We are therefore dressing up as something—garbed with discourses that categorically regard an enemy in each of us. It's a uniform to be worn. And, supposedly, the enemy is upon us. It's potentially anyone and everyone. The enemy cannot always be seen. To make this clear, everyone is distinguished and separated, perhaps agreeably and mutually segregated at the moment. Is the classic Leo Straussian neoconservative theory to blame here? With hopes of shoring up traditions and binding societal institutions it turns upon the self with its battle cry, "One always needs an enemy!"

Maybe there is something more intangible going on, which why Friedrich Nietzsche decided to make war with "a revaluation of all values," essentially, a war with every thought, every idea, and every idolized object past, present, and future. [20] He was simply brave, stupid, or mad enough to put forth the possibility by simply saying that "there are more idols than realities in the world."[21] Regardless, this unreality continues, trends, and is accepted with great and wondrous normalcy.

Opinion-making could be a misnomer, however. One seems to commit to boundary, to promise, to engage with the feeling of individualistic expressions. Opinion also becomes part of the social philosophies that protect the collective mind, the hive, the herd, yet at the same time presents a delusional notion that the individual is real, original, and the one who is truly right if and only if she or he lies subject to the group. Adversaries and opponents are sought out to economically feed into the antagonistic game play unifying and solidifying group and opinion-making back upon each other through great cyclical reoccurrences and reciprocity.

Even Ayn Rand warned us against the potential co-opting of opinion and stances—all at the expense of individual abstraction and expressiveness. Morality and ethics are indeed given a special autonomy released from convictions. Such is found in individual decision-making that only kneels to the caution of hasty overgeneralization of something so vaguely rationalized to begin with because in their "frantic desire to belong," said Rand, "they hope that the tribe will tell them *how to live.*" They regenerate a moral autonomy that becomes dangerously surrendered to a false conception, a collectivity where "any witch doctor, guru, or dictator" may provide the answers, may apply their control, or at least tell them what to do with their lives.[22]

The opinion produces, generates, reproduces, expands, and enters a bureaucratic realm.

The opinion is a repetitious production of values dispensed daily from its grouping centers—often sent out as mass emails, talking points, policies, procedures, orders, customer demographics, advertisements, likes, posts, uploads, and marketing schemes that display clothed and shielded activities—performances awaiting to be initiated from its command.

2

Commanding

The formula of my happiness: a Yes, a No. a straight line, a goal.

—Friedrich Nietzsche[23]

Consider the command structure of a sporting event for a moment. Let's say research observations were conducted on the sidelines and meticulously recorded. Factoring out gestures and body language, most audible linguistic displays pertain to yelling and shouting at the players on the field.

Here is an example transcript:

Spectator 1: Get the ball!

Spectator 2: Go! Go! Go!

Spectator 3: Hey! Watch out! Cover him!

Spectator 4: Come on [inaudible name]! Let's go! Get in the game!

Now let's consider the daily activities of work life. Let's suppose an average American will spend well over forty hours per week in such an environment.

Once more, an exemplified transcript:

Worker 1: Can you hand me the [inaudible tool or item] ?

Worker 2: Hey! Get over here and help us with this!

Worker 3: Look at this for me and make sure I'm doing it right.

Worker 4: Watch out! They're coming through here!

Worker 5: Make sure you show up at that meeting at 6 p.m.

Worker 6: Be quiet! [inaudible name of supervisor] is watching us right now.

Worker 7: How about you do your job and leave me alone?

Whether the statement is made with a smile or not, factoring out all facets of nonverbal communication, these are commonly accepted as commands.

There's a basic phenomenal pattern to our linguistic assertions. Charles Sanders Peirce called it an "ideal assertability." Any linguistic assertion requires an answer in thought, jest, activity, or otherwise.[24] Johann Gottlieb Fichte once described it as "the summons."[25] Brief utterances and snippets hold sway upon us as something imperative to our thinking and doing. At times none of these statements is logical really. Aristotle mentioned that apophantic discourse—what we now call logic or reason—brings something to light. This is a discourse that manifests a kind of truth, a truth subject to logical and instrumental relations. Command does not necessarily fall into the same category of discourse, and neither, I would argue, does opinion anymore.

Giorgio Agamben noted that "Aristotle's decision to exclude non apophantic discourse from philosophy has marked the history of Western logic."[26] Aristotle lists these excluded discourses in his *Poetics*: discourses "like prayers, commands, threats, narrations, questions and responses, exclamations, greetings, advice, curses, blasphemy, etc."[27] Apophantic discourse must take on a logical formation of productivity. It's a tool or exteriority devising about a truth relation, verification, yes/no, open/close, or the categories of modality, relation, possibility and so forth—a discourse to manifest and lighten up something (*phainōs*).

Aristotle does not end his analysis of the discourses here.

Ironically, in *Rhetoric* he places logic almost completely on the back burner. The dialectic of truth is secondary and set aside. What's more important is to set position against an opponent, and most importantly, incite an audience. They too must be wrangled by a discourse that steers their passions. "These emotions are pity, indignation, anger, hatred, envy, emulation, and pugnacity."[28] At the very base of Western logic is a doubling off, an awareness of truth versus an awareness of discourses outside of it: Something sets up and barrages its opposition and also incites and entangles the audience within this chasm.

In *Poetics,* character is a quality. Activities such as tragedies are an "imitation not of persons but of action and life."[29] The audience could lend us to what Hannah Arendt once interpreted as *theatai,* or "spectators." To the point though, Aristotle observed a qualitative distinction—a separate realm between action and activity. "All human happiness or misery takes the form of action—the end for which we live is a certain activity not a quality."[30] Further, he noted that a "character in a play is that which reveals the choice of agents."[31] This choice is imitatively played out and performed, "hence there is no room for character in a speech or a purely indifferent subject."[32] Activities and performances become a series of imitation routines.

Would if we were all merely rendered into the mode of acting? Not action, but activity, not authentic selfhood, but a character—qualities for analysis, imitative features, practices, abilities, gaming, and playing? What we consider action isn't so. It isn't choice; it's just picking, selecting, and meandering through a menu—a preselected menu of commands.

There may be only preferences among vast selections of generic commands.

Something commands the will.

Enter Friedrich Nietzsche: "to will is to command; inherent in Will is the commanding thought." Martin Heidegger noted that "no characteristic phrase occurs more frequently in Nietzsche."[33] The command has become the preeminent form of utterance that supersedes speech and discourse. A forty-hour work week is a labor activity that relies on a command structure. Yet also there is a technocratic no-nonsense practicality to it—to quickly act always at the forefront of every interaction: the proverbial "get to the point." Through these activities, command lays waste to speech, discourse, and dialogue where the latter occurs as a counter with the former.

In such scenarios as our transcripts imply, there are pure mental expressions of commands laden with imperatives: Will you? Won't you? Not you. Go there. Do this. And there are responses: He is. She is. I am. There are. We will. Yes, sir. Yes, ma'am. In the modulation of these utterances are nuances galore. Hence the command "Go!" is modified by its responses. The modal verbs: I can, I must, I will. This modification, according to Agamben, is what fashions and signifies an acceptance, the place where command and obey occur. These modal verbs placed together—I can, I must, I will—do not require an exact truth or articulation of any ethics whatsoever. Do they?

> When we hear the fatuous password 'I can' repeated so often today, it is likely that, in the decomposition of every ethical experience that defines our time, what the delirious person actually means to say is rather: 'I must will to be able,' that is:
> 'I command myself to obey.' [34]

Command and obey become merely acceptance and compliance through activity and performance.

What is a command?

The command may be traced back to the Greek term *archē*, which has two meanings: (1) origin, principle and (2) command, order. The derivative *archo* means to begin prior to something, and *archōn* literally means "the one who begins."[35] The command, according to Aristotle, is not part of apophantic discourse; it's not indicative and therefore lies in the realm of imperatives.[36] If it were indicative, it could be scrutinized and subjected to notions such as truth, falsity, interpretation and nuances of meaning, if not to a logical and rational assessment. Indicative language is language in the realm of philosophy and science. However, as the ancient Greek word suggests, the *archē*, along with its derivative, shows up as power beyond itself, the name for ancient city rulers, mystical beings depicted by the Gnostics, and a term for the very beginning and origins of the cosmos, the moment of creation itself given forth by God by theological interpretations. Thus the command imperative, as Agamben puts it, is a language in the realm of law, religion, and magic.[37]

All of this to sidestep the will that commands.

Was Nietzsche right? Agamben seems to think so. In other words, the will is nothing other than a command, "and that which the will commands is nothing other than potential."[38] The command renders potential inoperative. Work manifests, but only as it drains potential and collects activities, lays out generic markers, qualifiers, a menu to select a preference from. The will takes away the notion of can or cannot and replaces it with obedience. It's daunting once we begin to factor back into our scenarios such things as body language and technological apparatuses. The opinionated laden will makes "subjects who use them believe themselves to command them (and in fact push buttons defined as 'commands'), but in truth do nothing but obey a command inscribed in the very structure of the apparatus."[39]

Let's go a step further.

The command orders.

Its response assumes a pure mode of activity, or perhaps performativity, where there is a non reflective speculative event. It is doing, making one do, and making things do. What is lost to the Western tradition is perhaps the emphasis on the study and analysis of the indicative. As such, these "free citizens of democratic-technological societies are beings who incessantly obey in the very gesture with which they impart the command."[40] The device, tool, and online instrument are apparatuses that order. Taking orders is just like ordering food, and ordering ourselves in that very workplace are orders to be taken by customers, to obey orders in a command structure, to relay orders, to command and will upon and by each other. Even in the mode of temporary contemplation, in workplace activity or increasingly in leisure activity are activities in regard to the order, or to fashioning product, and the planning to bring obedience and a performative aspect with it.

Now we have a context to opinionated command statements. "You're wrong." "I'm right." The context of the highly competitive and oppositional utterance, "I win!" eventually commands and orders you into "You lost," "You are an object of my winning," or "You can't do this" the proverbial "You," the "object" of my willing, moving, manipulation, and mastery. There is a real sociological motivation behind it, and we can't really pin point to antagonistic gaming only. Mastery of anything appears moot once it begins to fuel and drive sociological aspects such grouping, uniting, and getting over the "object"—the opponent.

We can no longer traditionally describe any of this as "opinion-making."[41] As Hannah Arendt once noted, in its ancient conception, opinion (*doxa*) was usually coupled with fame and gain. In our two scenarios—the sporting event and the workplace—there are areas ridden by spectators and actors. Opinion does not become a discourse searching for truth because, once meshed with a highly competitive nature, it begins to couple and combine with command.

Here at this moment we would have to reluctantly suggest something.

Opinion is now packaged with command.

It is marketed, ordered, and parceled into directives, modes, and techniques.

Opinion is the "proto culture"[42] commanding our daily lives?

Clearly there are utterances and assertions that order us and summon obedience and compliance. They are obeyed by compliance, by allowing them to be said in the first place with the performative, mimicking, and activity-laden response. Or it is compliance by performance; the obeying is a response that was the intent all along—the necessity to oppose and conflict with an enemy of some kind.

3

The Opponent

Everything in him is exaggerated, *buffo,* a caricature; everything is at the same time concealed, ulterior, subterranean.

—Friedrich Nietzsche[43]

Friedrich Nietzsche once spoke of the conditions during the era of Socrates. He said, "Neither Socrates or his patients had any choice."[44] In a sense, they all had to be rational or perish. Socrates knew he was not alone. The old Greek ways were degenerating; "old Athens was coming to an end."[45] In his lifetime "degeneration was developing everywhere."[46] Socrates, according to Nietzsche, was part of the lowest class. He was a pleb, and infamous for his ugliness. He was a monstrosity that reflected his position in society. Socrates, therefore, was part of a unique contest, "he discovered a new kind of *agon,*"[47] a highly competitive nature with a new twist. At times Socrates would position his dialectic as if he were avenging something, or in utter violent revenge against the old noble ways of Athens. Nietzsche asked, "Does he, as one oppressed, enjoy his own ferocity in the knife-thrusts of his syllogisms? Does he *avenge* himself on the noble people whom he fascinates?"[48] Socrates took this "agonistic impulse"[49] of the Greeks and put it on steroids. His dialectic reeks of a monstrosity and complete, utter violence. At times he wrestled with the divine and noble ideas as a "variation of wrestling matches between men and youth."[50] Socrates was erotically disposed to the contest, and at odds with authorities for trying to get the youth on his side.

Socrates promoted a new brand with his contests, a new "personal artifice of self-preservation."[51] The decline of his society was the same degeneration that cornered him, where the only thing left is giving speech. Something had to give Socrates material to innovate, however. Once "the impulses want to play the tyrant; one must invent a counter tyrant who is stronger."[52] Regardless, something had to become the tyrant.

The tyrant had to be reason.

Socrates wielded the weapons of reason as a warrior and champion. "One must have to *enforce* one's right; until one reaches that point, one makes no use of it."[53] His onslaught was the dialectics. "As a dialectician, one holds a merciless tool in one's hand; one can become a tyrant by means of it; one compromises those one conquers."[54] His one-on-one contest, matching and counteracting with more than one partner, was not only a totalizing force of reason used as a weapon, but often an awkward erotic way to wrestle his opponent as if playing and tinkering with them at the same time. "The dialectician leaves it to his opponent to prove that he is no idiot: he makes one furious and helpless at the same time. The dialectician renders the intellect of his opponent powerless."[55] In the end, Socrates makes everyone into a fool and idiot, and they love him for it. He is loved because he conquers and disarms them to the point of helplessness, where the only help is the assistance of his philosophy, of him and none other.

Would if the contest is reduced and stripped to its bareness and the need for elongated dialectical displays diminished? We are simply reduced to the active measures of our abilities, and often a tactical ability to command. To command the will or to will around someone else is victory. Quick-witted utterances or abrupt movements are now the "Maxims and Arrows,"[56] the start, the end, and resurgences of short rhetorical jabs.

Are we stuck in this activity?

Are we caught up in the performative realm of jabbing, retorting, commanding, and quick-witted remarks?

This is a place where reality does not completely come to light; it's only performed. Giorgio Agamben suggested that, long ago, the relation between words and things was never distinguished. This ancient form of language was expressed during an "epoch when the relation between words and things was not apophantic, but instead had the form of command."[57] The words were unified with thing and both were subject to an arch, a command of it. Now we command one another. Stuck with words and things, we have separated ourselves just as if we were tools and devices. No truth to light but command that opposes one another while pushing, pulling, manipulating, and covering over the "real."

The tensions and tethers are felt in proximity. It cannot be explained or fully reduced to consciousness. No imagery can complete the picture.[58] Therefore no words can completely describe, nor would they need to, because elongated language prevents mimicry and performance it seems.

Aristotle's *Rhetoric* not only distinguishes non apophantic discourse, but here also he has done something rather curious. Rhetoric is persuasion relegated to the art of command and the itemization of the "opponent."[59] This begs some serious questions. Aristotle was already aware that rhetoric as a kind of discourse does not necessarily bring the thing or word into light; it does not manifest a logical ascertainable reality. In fact, he plays with this possibility. To be clear, Aristotle suggested that the base of the speech contained a logical presentation of truth. The remainder of the speech, however, should be directed at an opponent, and at the emotive content of an audience. The content of the speech must always have an enemy; there is to be an opposition, a tension, and mode of permanent contest.[60]

Under command, or avoidance of being commanded by a contesting or contentious opponent, is once again a place that does not bring reality to light, it does not ever completely manifest it. What command does is bring about performance, the place of opposition between words and things, where the "opponent" is part of the rhetorical device—an extension of the performative activities. By proxy, reality and each other become subjected to manipulation. The "opponent," says Aristotle, is not made untruthful or truthful, but is made into an extension and manipulation of the sentiments by which the audience becomes disposed. "You must make the audience well-disposed towards yourself and ill-disposed towards your opponent."[61]

Aristotle's "opponent," as he states, must be trounced. You have to make yourself out as the good man and your opponent as the bad one. One of the most important parts of rhetoric is bombardment of the opponent. This is not only a manipulation, but also a purposeful effect on the sentiments of the hearers, whereby the oratory event is to incite the audience's emotion in response to oppositional attacks. "These emotions are pity, indignation, anger, hatred, envy, emulation, and pugnacity."[62]

Rhetoric has to be language-open, however. As a persuasive art, it has to flourish without bounds. "For the true and the approximately true are apprehended by the same faculty; it may also be noted that men have a sufficient natural instinct for what is true."[63]

Because rhetoric is the "counterpart of dialectic," it is used by everyone. Logical notions do not fully apply, and for this reason rhetoric does not "belong to any definite science."[64] Rhetoric is between modality and possibility, and somewhere else altogether. It reaches and breaches the heights in another realm. As an art it arouses our emotions. The rhetorical arts incite "prejudice, pity, anger, and similar emotions that have nothing to do with the essential facts, but are merely a personal appeal to the man who is judging the case."[65]

Because "we must use, as our modes of persuasion and argument, notions possessed by everybody,"[66] rhetoric has to remain necessarily open to an interpretive art. "Consequently, if rules were laid down," there would be no art, no ability to open up into varying forms of persecutions, limitations, or suppressions, and thus "such people would have nothing to say."[67] At this moment we begin to notice a mystical Aristotle. Subtly, he began bringing words and practicing activities in-between thoughts and passions. Mediating between these faculties had to be something indescribable.

Something else has to be mentioned that will be further elaborated later on.

Hannah Arendt was convinced that *proairesis*, a term that Aristotle essentially made up, was "the precursor of the will," [68] a proto concept to Immanuel Kant's practical reason.[69] Something had to mediate between reason (*logos*) and desires. Something teeter totters between thinking and practicing to help bring about the choosing. "What actually happens is that, reason and desire being in conflict, the decision between them is a matter of 'preference,' of deliberate choice."[70]

We never realize how mystical Aristotle was until we liken his observations to something invariably and infinitely indescribable—mediating between reason and passion—as an interaction with an opponent. Rhetoric and Poetry seem to be doing something between the realms of reason and passion, thinking and activity.

4

My Truth Must Win

The victorious cause pleased the Gods, but the defeated one
pleases Cato.
—Cato[71]

Michel Foucault's *Society Must Be Defended* issues out a daunting story.
It explains that truth is not only won by the victors, but that the very
way in which knowledge is disseminated and compiled happens through
winning. Being the victor means that truth is the modality of
conquering.

Reason, the logical argument, is based on battle.

Affirmation only affirms a power over someone; the ability to gather
more resources and discipline over others issues out knowledge and
truth. If history were a positive crystallization, or if we could look of
any of this positively, there is indeed a gathering of knowledge of some
kind—even if only knowing the enemy.

Winning against an opponent, as Aristotle once described, happens
in front of an audience; this means that there is a need to gather
knowledge about both. Even in complete and utter warfare is a
primordial knowing of the other. Following the "essentials of victory,"
Sun Tzu mentioned how important knowledge of the enemy is.
Knowledge of oneself is equally important.

If you know the enemy and know yourself, you need not fear
the result of a hundred battles. If you know yourself but not
the enemy, for every victory gained you will also suffer a
defeat. If you know neither the enemy nor yourself, you will
succumb in every battle.[72]

Foucault's historical analysis centers on discursive practices that appear engaged in a battling motif. What he found was that the quest for truth and right is a discourse laden with a specific kind of power and authority, one that resembles war, victory, defensiveness, and conquest.

> The subject who speaks in this discourse is in battle; he has adversaries, and he fights for victory. No doubt, he tries to make right prevail, but the right in question is his particular right, marked by a relation of conquest, domination, or antiquity: rights of triumphant invasions or millennial occupations.[73]

This is a reality as much as it is a powerfully assertive victory. It's a phenomenon whereby someone, something, or an exemplified concept becomes an assertion of "a truth that functions as a weapon."[74] This is why history and rationality grow and develop alongside notions such as "calculations and strategies,"[75] and seem to win out and dominate because they display components of defense, tactic, and battle. This is a kind of "rationality that, as one rises and it develops," it also "becomes increasingly fragile, more and more spiteful," not to mention "more closely tied to illusion, to fancy, and to mystification."[76]

Foucault makes clear what a tactical type of discursive practice does.

> We are dealing, moreover, with a discourse that turns the traditional values of intelligibility upside down. An explanation from below, which is not the simplest, the most elementary, the clearest explanation but, rather, the most confused, the murkiest, the most disorderly, the most haphazard.[77]

If these are the explanations of reality that must be accepted as belief or fact, they are set up for battle because they are simultaneously the most haphazard, the most unclear, and if examined thoroughly, perhaps unfeasible. What this does, really, is to serve its purpose: perpetuate the battle, fight, and conflict for a type of discourse that arguably makes no sense. In other words, it perpetuates a defense rather than an argument that would eventually flesh out any semblance of fact or knowledge. Foucault continues, "What is meant to serve as a principle of decipherment is the confusion of violence, passions, enmities, revenges; it is also the web of petty circumstances that decide defeats and victories."[78]

In the end, this is a discourse that lives in symbiosis with the concept of war. This is a "discourse which deciphers the continued existence of war in society." It is an antagonism within a unique "historico-political discourse" that constructs given "truth functions used as a weapon for a partisan victory, a discourse at once darkly critical and intensely mythical."[79]

The historical actor speaks of subjects. He must subject his object, parceled and packaged, to what is deemed "truth" and "right." This actor wishes to constitute himself through the tactics and strategies given by the rhetoric of war. "Of course, he speaks the discourse of right, asserts a right and demands a right,"[80] although delving ever closer to an assertion mimicking and acting out battles.

> These are singular rights, and they are strongly marked by a relationship of property, conquest, victory, or nature. It might be the right of his family or race, the right of superiority or seniority, the right of triumphal invasions, or the right of recent or ancient occupations.[81]

A discourse manifesting rights has to be fought for and won. Right manifested into "truth" may be something else entirely. In other words, "right" and "true" may not be synonymous except through powering and commanding.

What becomes the itemization of "truth" and "right" merely represents a public discourse of force. "The truth, is, in other words, a truth that can be deployed only from its combat position, from the perspective of the sought-for victory and ultimately, so to speak, of the survival of the speaking subject himself."[82] That is not all. Our modern conceptions of history and philosophy appear to be premised upon this "battle."

From the ancient Greek era to the Middle Ages, from the dominance of church and nobility to the seventeenth and eighteen centuries of French and American revolutions, eventually a "historical discourse developed and became a tactical instrument, a sort of discursive weapon that could be used by all the adversaries present within the political field."[83] Instruments, tactics, strategies, and defense of the speaking subject came together and eventually developed the idea of a "constitution."[84] Further, Foucault notes that this mode of discursive battling is what developed the modern philosophical era. "The philosophy of history as philosophy of cyclical time becomes possible once the two notions of a constitution and a relationship of force become established."[85]

Let's accept the premise that rational calculation is now autonomous. Thinking and activity are relegated to imitations, qualities of characters, performances, and commands. Do we now observe a highly competitive era laden with transaction and exchanges, where thinking is reduced into pure doing?

What shall we say of opinion?

Opinion-making is highly competitive, team-oriented, unified and sociologically appearing through antagonistic gaming at the same time. Truth and victory are possessions and the spoils of war. "My" truth must win. "My" belief must be victorious. Opinion is more than just belief; it is the battle ground of right and wrong, of winning and beating expressed in activities. The winning, losing, lost, and defeated are translated into a pure game of "truth" and "right," where the victors win the opinion. The losers must therefore hide their opinion constantly covering over of those internal feelings perpetuating a defensive posture once more.

Let's reflect on to the Socrates that Friedrich Nietzsche once interpreted—the man who felt it necessary to turn *reason* into a tyrant."[86] The mighty character, Socrates, who was merely part of a political, vengeful, and rebellious movement against the degeneration of his civilization thereby erotically wrestling with the youth so he could teach them to take their own jabbing, thrusting, and rebellious blows against the decadence of a tyrannical nobility in decline. The thought of a Socrates who presented a cure for these societal and philosophical ills with "his own personal artifice of self-preservation"[87] is quite marvelous and fanciful, if not completely a phantasm.

Perhaps it is now made clear to us. This historical process of thinking, the *psyche* and its fictions we make to cure our thoughts, is instead actually reevaluating and reordering values. Maybe this is why Friedrich Nietzsche, in *The Twilight of the Idols,* decided to declare war on everything.[88]

5

The Logical Game without End

They'll spend their whole lives hating and being hated, plotting and being plotted against, more afraid of internal than of external enemies, and they'll hasten both themselves and the whole city to almost immediate ruin.

—Plato[89]

Let's take the Socratic contest to its agonistic extremes for a moment. The Socratic plebeian revolt against the decline and degeneration of a noble Athenian way of life begins to vengefully posit reason as the tyrant. We shall find that a tyrant or group of tyrants eventually become tyrants themselves. They too develop reasons to be such, and must legitimize their positions.

As irrational as this may seem, there's logic in this kind of game.

Let's begin with some basic symbolic logical modes: modus, meaning "mood." Modus Ponens, from the Latin *ponere* means to affirm, i.e., the "affirmative mood,"[90] symbolically expressed this way: If P then Q, P, therefore Q. The subject P is affirmed, thereby affirming the consequential relationship with Q. We also need to present Modus Tollens, from the Latin *tollere*, "to deny,"[91] symbolically expressed this way: If P then Q, Not Q, therefore Not P. The denial of the consequent disallows the affirmation of the subject. This mood of denial is a negative move objectively found once the consequent is negated, which in turn negates the subject.

Our dissension and subversion happen in the production and thereby negation against each other.

Walter Benjamin,[92] among others,[93] once suggested that material production must take the form of negation. The consequential goal is always a negation that becomes mass-produced: It is a massive mood of tollens. Even if we can't find a complete etymological or semantic relation with "tolling,"[94] it is the toll that taxes us. The ancient Greek notion derived from Anaximander is *taxis,*[95] which eventually obscures any logical notion of cause. Fated history as object or thought is only relationally seen as paying debt to a prior relation, mostly time. So it becomes an "order of and retribution, debt and payback."[96] The consequent denies the subject wherever it goes.

Guilt is produced, refreshed, and reproduced.

At the very basic levels of symbolic logical productivity, externalization eventually meets either the ponens or tollens. The basic externalization of anything must avoid negation, a mood of denial. Exportation, for example, is a tautology where If P and Q then R is equal to If P then (If Q then R),[97] therein if R is negated according to the mood of denial, then so too is the entirety of what is produced and externalized.

Material productivity as a form of negation is therefore a denial at the basic level of production. Exportation and externalization, as the principle of negation, could take hold, thereby refreshing the subject.

It's a logical anti-logic.

The subject P has to refresh itself anew. In other words, If P then Q, Not Q; therefore P refreshes and renews into P 2.0 and starts over again to the next negation. If P 2.0 then R. R is negated. P 2.0 refreshes into P 3.0. If P 3.0 then S. S is negated, and P 3.0 refreshes. If P 4.0 then T...Refresh, negation, refresh, negation, rinse, wash, repeat, and so forth

There is a constant refreshing and renewal alongside a negation in the modes of production. Guilt, in its negative, makes us refresh ourselves and try again, produce more, buy more, an in the end, the consequent is negated, thus producing more guilt—and start over, negate, guilt, start again.

Material production as negation is the reason, according to Alexandre Kojève, there is no past. Rather, it is the end of history. "The end of history is nothing but the patient dialectical work of negation, and man is both the subject and the stakes in this negating action."[98] The present relation to the past is negated by a constant refresh, by a constant need to renew—a new sale, a new product, a new consideration, a new motivational goal that forces us into the next negation. "The end of history involves, then, an epilogue in which human negativity is preserved as a remnant."[99]

Now, instead of looking at the "mood" of productivity (logically, that is), and how this may be a separate scenario from a democratic mood, I wish to look at something else for a moment.

In specific instances and cases, basic logical negation is used as a political tool; subversion, conspiracy, and the bipolar logic of dualism are used as a modus operandi of governing political and corporate entities. If used properly it becomes a game—a game with high stakes, and a game that never ends.

Jaime Malamud-Goti once noted that Argentina's response to authoritarianism, a shift from a totalized societal and political dominance into democracy, became a massively contested game of political and juridical "hardball" so intense as to incite responses in kind—a retaliatory tit for tat.[100]

It makes us wonder: What about the other way around?

Does this transition from overt totalitarianism to democracy invert itself? Does a transition from an open democratic society into an extremely competitive, antagonistic gaming society let us observe, or at least gauge, the same thing—a "game without end?"[101]

Argentina becomes a wonderful case study in this regard.

In Argentina a series of groups and individuals forcibly took power and implanted their own brands of authoritarian regimes. Interestingly, according to Malamud-Goti, these regimes sustained themselves through negation logic, among other things.

The logic of conspiracy was upheld by the constant need for "self-sealing proofs."[102] For strength and legitimacy to be upheld, the affirmation of a negation had to be manifested. A foe-versus-ally logic began to present itself, whereby the "enemy" was rigidly defined. Hence "subversion" became the paramount political tactic compared to earlier historical cases among French Algerian situations, for example.

Here we observe P in a constant and stable reaffirmation, setting up and then continually negating its consequent.

Although resistances to authoritative regimes was unquestionably occurring, these resistances had to be labeled, defined, and logically manifested as an enemy of the governing body to legitimize it and strengthen its own affirmation. "Unlike terms such as *terrorist* or *insurgent* that denote organized mayhem, *subversive* does not necessarily indicate violent activity."[103] A subversive could be anyone, anything, or any thought, and thus span boundaries and continua between passive and aggressive. Someone could be labeled an enemy in a much broader way, even if they were not violent or active at all, thus strengthening the authoritarian arm. In this sense "subversion represented just the first step in a strategy of destabilization in which most actors, they thought, would later turn to sabotage and terrorism."[104] Thus, the "subversive" parties and groups could be deemed an opposition, an enemy, and could be acted upon as such even if they had not broken the law or acted out themselves.

Note that "subversion" is being defined along the lines of philosophy by Karl Popper,[105] where such a term is an "expression used by enemies of freedom—authorities who have almost always succeeded in persuading the guileless and well-meaning."[106] And so the language by which enemies are defined is invariably important, where they were once labeled with concepts such as "dissenter, traitor, or opponent," the difference between tolerable and intolerable feelings modulates the wording and terminology as such.[107]

What about the other way around?

What happens when the change is from open to closed, freedom to totality?

What is considered activity and passivity here?

This defining and redefining process of people and ideas clearly exhibits a chauvinistic character.[108] Character is of course a quality and thereby becomes parceled to an object to be moved about and manipulated. These are qualities that become externalized and produced as part of negation, guilt, and then refreshment. Characterizations occur in the midst of vast gaming of substitution and antagonism—never-ending games heightened by commands—commands coupled with what were once considered opinions. Antagonistic gaming as a form of substitution thereby presents a unification of opinion, thought, or activities generalizing and rendering individuals and groups into objects. While we command one another, our dialectical gaming is a series of substitution and proximal relations with the very objects we wish to will upon, i.e. one another.

The transference from open to closed, or the closing of what was once open, may indeed have gauges and barometers. According to Malamud-Goti the national philosophies, religions, and art begin to define our reality in terms of fatalism, acquiescence, and guilt.

What now do we have in terms of words and labels for each other?

The subversion premise must construct and redefine an opponent as dissenter, thereby self-sealing a totalizing position against the opponent. This conspiracy logic sets the tone and modulates the frequency by which a bipolar logic is set up. In other words, to make "subversion" impossible, to quell insurgency and dissenters there must be an increased production of refreshable naming of them and at the same time an increased identification and modulation between what is considered active and passive.

The names have to constantly change and modify to incite and refresh the negative premise. Certain ideas and groups must be fueled or enabled into frequencies of activity by a constant redefining of "bad," "mad," "not enough," "not capable," "not on our side," or quite simply the invariably negating "not," and refresh P 2.0, 3.0, 4.0, rinse, wash, and repeat. Certain political or societal values are defined only by the authoritative and positional request of these values, and they are also the ordering of values, the commanding, resetting, and situating of the modes of negation.

6

Opposition, or Substitution

Never am I less alone than when I am by myself, never am I
more active than when I do nothing.

—Cato[109]

Me—Not Me. What You say—My reaction to it. Mind/Society, Self/
Other, double—split—double—add—divide—add. One move at a
time and it still makes its move from one place to another place. Position
against—oppose—couple—oppose.

"Always the same metaphor," Hélène Cixous lamented. "We follow
it, and it carries us, beneath all its figures, wherever discourse is
organized."[110] Historical discourse is warfare and beyond. Once
submerged in a persistent war with concept, idea, person, place, group,
or thing the opposition plays itself out in such a complicated and yet
simple manner. "If we read or speak," claimed Cixous, "the same thread
or double braid is leading us throughout literature, philosophy, criticism,
centuries of representation and reflection."[111] No wonder Friedrich
Nietzsche declared war on all idols past, present, and future. Why not?

The dualism is irreconcilable.

It never completely resolves and never fully defines or explains itself.
Combat is the historical argument brought to fruition. The duality
posits our knowledge. Our history of thought is built upon this strife.

Through dual, hierarchal opposition. Superior/Inferior.
Myths, legends, books, Philosophical systems. Everywhere
(where) ordering intervenes, where a law organizes what is
thinkable by oppositions.[112]

Cixous points us toward coupling as an entry point to this oppositional dualism. "And all the pairs of opposites are *couples*," she said. Jacques Derrida once mentioned that an awareness of French idioms may be important, especially the way Cixous uses *tous les deux,* or "all the twos," or "all the duos"[113] as it may be interpreted. An ancient Platonic problematic of oneness (*hen*) plays out in this unique usage of the word "all," such that ancient Greek wisdom asks for "Peace as the return of the multiple to unity."[114] Cixous is saying "all" of the pairs, duos, coupling. "All" of them are at once contradictorily considered dual before we even try to arrive at our analysis of thought, value, and meaning—before we wish to begin to inscribe a reconciliation, resolution, or attempt to make it dissolve.

We must consider for a moment the basic premise that Cixous has laid out for us.

"Thought has always worked through opposition."[115]

Does this excuse activity?

Better yet, is it thinking that opposes itself and every facet of everything else?

Hannah Arendt once claimed that thinking, willing, and judging are irreducible to each other. Arendt said a proper mode of judgment bridges the divide between thinking and doing.[116] Emmanuel Levinas said that we must also consider something else from Plato, namely that "Same" and "Other" are irreducible to each other. From here the modern conception jumps off into a pervasive and "knowing I that is to be the melting pot of such a transmutation"[117] between Same and Other. With Cixous, however, it is much more simple and yet complex at the same time. Thinking as history and its manifested formations play out through an interplay between passivity and activity—passive/active coupling.

"All" of the logocentrisms, the conceptual systems, the binary, relate back to the couple, back to man—woman? Cixous lets thought duel it out with nature, just to prove the point, and almost in quasi-Hegelian moments. She goes through the vast and absolute duos, Nature/History, Nature/Art, Nature/Mind, then Passion/Action? Why do these two oppose? These do not couple? Why does Nature somehow transmute into Passion? Back to woman and man—where is passive and active? "And the movement whereby each is set up to make sense is the movement through which the couple is destroyed."[118] Opposition, obliteration, and abasement happen to the woman, and worse, they take hold as an appearance with no resolution.

The opposition from the couple—from man's symbolic authority is also his ability and necessitated as extension, ego, mind, production, and tooling. Luce Irigaray said man substituted with instrument, product, and tool. And women, in their coupling, must also substitute competitively with other women.[119] In men's public hold upon men's productivity, the application of instruments can be applied as an activity; is the avoidance or acceptance passivity?

Substitution is a discourse outside. It cannot be entirely rendered to imagery and manifesting language to be brought to light; it is felt and beyond felt. It has "incommensurability with regards to consciousness, a proximity that is absolute exteriority, a relationship with a singularity, without the mediation of any principle or ideality."[120] It merely posits its existence and demands to be recognized. Substitution is a proximal relation that distributes through oppositional discourse outside of how it reveals itself.

Are substitution and proximity interchangeably the organs of activity and passivity? Should we think of a moment that cannot be reduced to imagery? It reduces you to feeling its activity against your passive engagements, non thinkable to the image that your consciousness can bestow upon it. It replaces you with the currency of values, a monetization that isn't you. Oppositional othering engages in substitution processes. "You are this, this is you, I'm saying this about you, etc." The object of substitution engages your proximity.

This thought is you. This stance, this opinion, this like, this post—a menu to select from—data—trend—data.

If we read what Cixous and Emmanuel Levinas are saying bit more closely, then we begin to engage the ability to have non resoluble imagery that brings about proximity in the first place. What is felt can never fully be revealed nor described. Proximity must occur in the moment where imagery cannot be resolved. Considering that our language produces imagery for our thinking, the object/image, the externalized production of substitutive values is then used as the instrument to act back upon us. This proximal relation is a place—loosely described as a locality because it is neither geographic nor geometric—where being conscious of one another cannot be fathomed.[121] The ability to produce thematization cannot be derived or initiated.

So what of language that begins with imagery?

Hannah Arendt once had a side thought about this issue. In her discussion of Ludwig Wittgenstein's theory of language she points to our symbolic ordering and game play that begin to form imagery. Wittgenstein philosophically realized and became "aware of the hieroglyphic script, which depicts the facts that it describes."[122] Other languages and ways of communicating posit the image first. Does this happen before the thought? If we begin with image, does this resolve it? Where is thinking and activity? Where is the contemplative, the passive, the active? Arendt goes on,

> Yet language, the only medium through which mental activities can be manifest, not only to the outside world but also to the mental ego itself, is by no means as evidently adequate for the thinking activity as vision is for its business of seeing.[123]

I recall that Walter Benjamin once described a similar feature within our artifices, particularly architecture. This happens in a modality between sight and touch, perception and use. Architecture transfers activity to habit and then into distraction. "The distracted person, too, can form habits,"[124] so in this situation the optical is contemplation. Habit determines this optical reception. But in the end, the language must turn to touch. There has to be tactile appropriation. "For the tasks which face the human apparatus of perception at the turning points of history cannot be solved by optical means, that is, by contemplation alone."[125] Our visual appropriations—mentally, and in dialogue and discourse—eventually turn into habit, use, and tactile components. Visualization alone cannot seem to grasp nor master its constructions and artifices. It has to be felt, rendered, touched, held, the non-reducible consciousness of proximities. Hence it seems that dialectical imagery—as thinking, using, doing, and touching—are not only part of our activities; there's an issue between the proximal feeling felt by their substantive qualities we seem to deploy upon them.

Thinking must turn into doing, and sight (the speculative) into touch (the usage).

Something must substitute.

Is substitution itself at the base of opposition?

Is proximity?

Maybe Friedrich Nietzsche truly was on to something. His war on idols was a "revaluation of all values," because "there are more idols than realities in the world."[126] In other words, the secondary imagery of an identity is not a replacement; it is a substitutional phantasm for us to battle and oppose.

Now let us reassess the mystical side of Aristotle once more.

This cannot be fully elucidated without a few more of Aristotle's terms such as *dynamis* (potential), *energeia* (the manifested act), *facere* (fabrication), and *proairesis* (faculty of choice). Recall that Hannah

Arendt was convinced that the latter, *proairesis*, a term that Aristotle essentially made up, was "the precursor of the will," [127] a proto concept to Immanuel Kant's practical reason.[128] Something had to mediate between reason (*logos*) and desires. Something teeter totters between thinking and practices to help bring about the choosing. "What actually happens is that, reason and desire being in conflict, the decision between them is a matter of 'preference.' of deliberate choice."[129]

But what accounts for this imitative and performative character? Where do we find a nexus between action and activity?

We can look at *dynamis* and *energeia* for the answers. Potential is not only a stored energy that manifests if realized; it is also the ability not do something as well as do it. Aristotle's very essence of potential has to do with a "living being, who exists in the mode of potential, is capable of his own impotential, and only in this way does he possess his own potential. He can be and do because he preserves a relation with his own not being and not doing." [130] The ancient man was a "being of potential" wherein he can or cannot do something, in him "every potential is both potential to be and the potential not to be."[131] Modern man, however, became a "subject who *wills.*"[132] It gets even more interesting when we realize that Aristotle's term, *energeia,* the manifested act, (yet another word Aristotle conjured), is essentially the acting result of a potential doing or not doing, a can or cannot, the stored energy. What's crystallizing into activity is *energeia* derived from the Greek *ergon* (work). "In this context, *ergon* does not simply mean 'work,' but what defines *energeia*, the activity or being-in-act proper to human beings."[133] Potential in this regard becomes an inoperative remainder where *energeia* is not simply an act or action; it is the very activity proper to humans in that it is being, and therefore it defines ontology. [134] Therein Aristotle sets up his notion of happiness or the political being as a qualified life proper.

Here we discover the activity of work and potential as another mystical in-between feature itemized by active and passive.

Something has to lie between this thinking and doing. Arendt finds a solution from Duns Scotus. Somewhere in our sheer activity, purely expressing potencies and manifested working of them, is a fashioning and fabricating (*facere*). Man's artificial nature and his building and selecting among the doings with himself and the world become a series of transient operations. This may solve our character and quality issue for the moment (choice/action versus imitative activity/performance) if we realize that our thinking and practices have an array of transient occurrences.[135] That is, until we look at substitution and proximity.

The substitution becomes the character placed on us, the quality imitated and performed, a character that can be simulated—a not me—me, and a not you—you. It is an analogy being played out as culture, society, genre, brand, name, or object that someone says you are; it becomes a felt proximity. The substitution becomes the quality, or rather a quality is substituted as the entire proximal relation to your being. This can be rather freely felt, an always optional choosing between active and passive where the infinite and varying ability to substitute and enter into an array of proximal relations initiates indescribable expressiveness.

This can also be one's demise—or at least the continual perpetuation of oppositional duality.

Your identity becomes an aspect that is substituted without voluntary association—the quality, the character, the activity of a language that never fully comes to light. The quality becomes the opposition to play with, forced upon, the label, the name, the ability to render action as it begins to command rather than choose. Commanding the will becomes a tactical substitution to produce passivity. The only things left are picking, selecting, scrounging—not choice, just the passive activity of substitutive qualities called character and persona, labeled and applied as something imitative to thought, deed, desire, or the ability to name and define your world.

Where is *proairesis*? The great mediation between reason and desire becomes a greater divide between thinking and doing, potential and the manifest, active and rendering the opponent passive through infinite substitutions.

We have confused substitution with choice—picking, replacing, and commanding. The substituting event is the calling out and ordering of command, names that never completely manifest. They only present imperatives, logical or non logical analogies gone haywire that bring forth imitative activities of replacement. The replacement of things and the replacement of people becomes replacement for idea and object, the faculties of thought, and otherwise. If philosophy is the setting and ordering of values as both Nietzsche and Cixous suggested, then gauging where activity and passivity occur in then is ordering is very difficult. Because substitution, as Emmanuel Levinas once put it, is pure passivity.

Passivity becomes so passive it's active?

In the end, we produce and mass produce objects and thoughts that substitute for the previous. In the end, we wonder if this is activity or merely a renaming and reordering of the same oppositional problems.

With a glimmer and allusion, Cixous lamented,

Consulting the history of philosophy—since philosophical discourse both orders and reproduces all thought—one notices that it is marked by an absolute *constant* which orders values and which is precisely this opposition, activity/passivity.[136]

With coupling, the woman is nature.

Passion is sought as the memory of it, the ebbs and flows of the cosmos. The passive is stability, or is it active? Is active the flowing and ebbing, or is this passive? The allegory for our perception of nature, physics, and the universe is continuous. The passive forgetting is the most active in that it deactivates and starts the cycle anew. Passion and our reoccurrences looked at this way are at least the best scenarios that could get us away from oppositional and substitutional thinking altogether, correct?

7

My Stance
My Standing
My Critique of Status?

Nor must mothers, believing bad stories about the gods
wandering at night in the shapes of strangers from foreign
lands, terrify their children with them. Such stories blaspheme
the gods and, at the same time, make children more cowardly.

—Plato[137]

Apparently the ancient pre-Socratic Greeks fought so much and so often
that it became predicatively customary. Generational customs were
developed, and philosophical notions were born. Like clockwork, almost
likened to the rhythm of the seasons, city-states would proceed into
their quarrels and fights. The survivors would gather and take an oath to
Memory herself. It was an oath of amnesia. "The Athenian *amnēsta* is not
simply a forgetting or repression of the past; it is an exhortation not to
make bad use of memory."[138]

The ancient Egyptians were considerably more obvious about their
conflicts in this regard. It appears that battles between the Northern and
Southern Kingdoms happened so much and so often that they became
deified and systematized into their pantheon. Seth was the god known
for his antagonistic tangling within and without the lands of Egypt. He
may have originally been thought of as the "desert deity who came to
represent the forces of disturbance and confusion in the world."[139] He
was often described as a foreign god, however.[140] He was attributed

with the foreign deities from the Northern regions and the Eastern Delta.[141] Which deity Seth was associated with depended on the time period and reign of varying Egyptian dynasties. He has been linked with foreign rulers such as Baal,[142] and Seth's relatives and siblings were likened to foreign goddesses such as Anat and Astarte.[143] Robert Graves traced conquering Seth cults to the story of Gordium and King Midas[144]

What's clear is Seth's association to the unknown, chaos, deceit, and breaking of taboo.[145] The usurper god threatened its presence among the cycling seasons of the Nile—the god of violence, chaos, and confusion, sometimes even the god that "stood in the bow of the sun,"[146] other times the deity amid the chaotic and primordial cosmic serpent such as Apophis, or the later affiliations to Yam and even the Greek Typhon.[147] Over time, Seth became recognized as a natural opponent, as the manifestation of opposition itself. "As the god of chaos, he opposed the harmony of *maat* (truth) and was a dark side to the fabric of the universe."[148]

The ancients observed that all of this warring seemed natural. And the philosophy that developed was not only an aspect of how we perceive our being, but how the physical world actually works. "In the eyes of the Greeks, it was not possible to isolate the forces of discord from those of union culture in the web of human relationships or in the constitution of the world."[149] War was the nature of the cosmos. It was physics. It was the societal affairs of men with one another.

The ancient Greeks developed the term *stasis* to portray an oppositional tension. It appears to be the necessitated stability of the state, whereby its derivative is a state or condition, like actually being something, like status. Within the word *stasis* is a tensional meaning such as stability and permanence against a conflict or civil war. This stance that the ancients Greeks took in their varying city-states was a duty met with praise. So within this permanence is a fluctuating contentiousness. Here the subtle difference between the ancient and moderns must be noted. Stance was not an object; it was ethos, or worse, the permanent ebbs, flow, and cycles of the natural cosmos. Put simply, the Greeks could hardly speak of a "thing" at all,[150] thus an object standing and the way moderns consider it must be reconsidered as something such as cosmic stability and instability—and beyond this.

Plato discussed it often. Hans-Georg Gadamar points out that Plato's *Theaetetus* uses *stasis* as the key concept to describe, flux, flow, permanence, and stability at the same time. In this dialogue there is a unique wordplay. There are

> two positions placed opposite each other like two combatants: on the one side, the *rheontes,* those who are for flux and maintain the eternal flux of things, and, on the other side, the *stasiôtai,* a wordplay designating those who, like "rebels," take a stand on the immobility of that which exists and in this respect are revolutionaries at the same time.[151]

In its very vernacular the notion *stasiôtês* not only "means the same thing as revolutionary" but also is regarded as "the taking of a stand against the predominant view of the general flux." Gadamer added "when one insists on the identity of being, the permanent, and the constancy of being, this truly is a revolution." [152] This becomes an allegory about being and *physis.* Plato intended to use *stasis* to mean taking a stand and simultaneously rebelling, as a notion of permanence and fluctuation—cosmically and naturally observed. Gadamer further held that "it is crucial that the confrontation over the meaning of being is carried out between two points of view in a manner similar to the dispute between that which flows (*rheontes*) and that which is permanent (*stasiôtai*)."[153] There's no doubt Plato was using prior customs, words, and slang to make his philosophical points on these matters.

Nicole Loraux provided an analysis of civil war (*stasis*) in ancient Greece. She placed it in a relationship between the family/household economies (*oikos*) and the city-state (*polis*). Plato's *Menexenus* is the prime example.

Giorgio Agamben points out that this particular Platonic dialogue contains a purposive oxymoronic statement, "war at home," or *oikeios polemos*. Plato's literary move is observed in the word *polemos*, which usually implies external conflicts. Here is how it reads to those keeping score:

> Our war at home was waged in such a fashion that were fate to condemn humanity to conflict, no one would wish to see their city suffer this predicament in any other way. With such joviality and familiarity did those from the Piraeus and those from the city engage with one another.[154]

Once again, in using such artistic license the statement "war at home" is also met with "joviality and familiarity." "The factional bond moves into the household to the same extent to which the family bond is estranged in the faction."[155] In this sense there is an external conflict described as a war at home met with joy and familiarity. To add to the contradiction is the idea of familiarity (*to syggenēs*), or "the family bond." Its derivatives—*genos*, genus, gene, generation—denote that familial relations are at war in a constant revolving and cyclical positioning. That is why war is met with such joviality: It is expected and revered.

The war is met with celebration because it brings into fruition reconciliation for another generation. It's already done before it begins. And it seems that every Greek was raised into the honor of bringing about this war with each other as if it were a ceremonial custom, a rite of passage. Agamben and Loraux note that "Plato seems to imply that the Athenians had waged an internecine war only in order to better reconvene in a family celebration with one another."[156] In *Republic*

Plato wrote that they "fight among themselves as if they were fated to be reconciled."[157] Regardless, the wording of *oikeios polemos*, external or foreign war, is another clever way of describing *stasis*, or civil war, without literally mentioning it.[158]

A brief analysis of the etymology of *stasis* is quite revealing and somewhat incomplete unless we try to think about it in regard to other philosophical and sociological traditions. The word derives from *histemi* which means the act of rising, otherwise denoted as standing firmly upright. The *stas* was the one who swears while standing. [159] The derivative *stasimos* was traditionally the chorus in Greek tragedies which would stand. The chorus also provided prolonged and continuous singing, denoting permanence or at least the incremental ordering of duration. This chorus gave a pattern and sequence that permeated as the backdrop of the tragedy, thereby contributing to the story itself. The chorus also imitated a spectator of some kind, a constancy of observation within the backdrop of the play.

Further, historian Daniel J. Boorstin noted that ancient festivals that incorporated the "chorus" and the "orchestra" are where we find ritualistic dancing in circles exhibited "for the shared communal experience which was overwhelming. The chorus came before the solo."[160] This circular dancing noted the communal participation of cycles that happened ever concentric to the area of the orchestra—the marketplace—the place eventually delegated to the image of a god.

> These outdoor celebrations were open to the sky. In Athens they were later moved from the agora (marketplace) where everyone took part, to the southern slope of the Acropolis, where too the nucleus was an "orchestra," a circular dancing place around the altar of the god. The dithyrambs sung and danced there came to be known as "circular" dances for a "circular" chorus.[161]

In this place near the orchestra was the area where the god could witness the festival. "Except for the god there were no spectators."[162]

Delving further into the Greek lexicon, we find several contexts such as rebel, revolt, rising rebellion, to dispute, to divide into factions, political factions, party, strife, sedition, as well as standing, posture, post, station. And, from the Latin "status" "the state or condition in which a person is," come standing, stationary, and stable. [163]

Taking a stance or standing was a sign of permanence, stability and structure in this coming of age—a glorified rite of tensions that ordered being designated to a given locale. The Greeks portrayed that the very moment of being—considered here as rebelliousness, seditiousness, oppositional tensions, and conflict—were literal moments of civil war. This stance-taking in the city as political was ironically an expected permanence, and inversely a process. "They depict all of this as a process, whereas the problem consists primarily in comprehending the meaning of being."[164] We must recall, as Gadamer did, that what is actually being described is an exemplar story of the nature of being itself, *physis,* and the cosmos depicted as a dispute over *rheontes,* "that which flows," and *stasiôtai,* "that which is permanent."

This is further complicated by Solon's laws. Here citizens are punished by *atimia* and lose their rights as citizens if they do not fight on a side or take a stand during a civil war. If a citizen does not take a stance, he is expelled from the city and confined to the household therefore "losing citizenship by being reduced to the unpolitical condition of a private person." [165] Once again we find the notion of "stasis" in the sense that it "determines for itself the political and unpolitical character of a certain being."[166] Thus we find citizenship, rights, and duties defined through an oppositional indifference, a contradictory, if not oxymoronic polemic of identity and status found in a simultaneous permanence and tensional flux. Being is defined and positioned with a circular dance of flux and permanence within a state: This is me standing so as to fight for or against.

Identity is the position to be fought and defended, the stance of permanent contestation. Identity contends. Being rebels. This is a status of stability and strife, flux and permanence that solidified the bonds of the household economies and state. In this standing, positioning, and strife is a "field of tensions"[167] between familial bonds and state political bonds, the private and public sphere—significant others and generalized others, or even more to the point, the interplay between the "static" relations of the family as domestic production and the state or polis, or the very "statuses" of who we think we are.

Now in this context we must take another look at this sociologically and philosophically while shying away from the etymology of "status" and "stasis."

There's another approach.

Let's drop back to Plato's literary move for a moment.

From another angle we can suggest that, although Plato was conducting a social commentary and history, he was no sociologist. However, what Plato was doing was perhaps a proto sociology to arrive at the nature of physical reality and ontology.

From this perspective let's look at the basis of Max Weber's sociology for a moment. Weber deployed "ideal types."[168] Weber had to develop a strategy to find regularities in a chaotic social milieu, ever-constant observable features reduced to social action. The social or historical observer must thereby scientifically construct among the chaos something that can be averaged or generalized, or some sort of causal relationship that can stand against a "pure" idea—a typified indication that can, at least in thought, situate within the fabric of being. The idea happens purely in a vacuum, a laboratory thought design that can contend with the chaotic flux of infinite social relations and values. Hence Weber was primarily concerned with meaning as a possible constant; the very comprehension of *evidenz* is based on constancy, stability, and permanence. He was also adamantly aware that his "pure type" must address flux and change happening among social phenomena.

> The subjective meaning of a social relationship may change, thus a political relationship once based on solidarity may develop into a conflict of interests. In that case it is only a matter of terminological convenience and of the degree of continuity of the change whether we say that a new relationship has come into existence or that the old one continues but has acquired a new meaning. It is possible for the meaning to be partly constant, partly changing. [169]

Weber, concerned greatly with meaning, describes two kinds of meaning. The first is the actual actor or plurality of actors in the chaotic flux of the social, political, and historical milieu. The second is the pure type attributed to a "hypothetical actor or actors."[170] The observation is placed upon a "subjective meaning of a social relationship that may change."[171] Thus it is quite possible for meaning to always be considered "partly constant and partly changing."

Weber was not alone.

His friend and colleague Georg Simmel's quest for a "pure sociology" was a bit of a "cosmic tragedy" that proceeded with the assumption that "forms are merely injected into social life."[172] A commentator noted that Simmel "wished to reserve sociology for the task of checking both stagnation and the premature articulation of other items."[173] In his discussion of faithfulness and gratitude, Simmel described how celebratory fervor shows "a basic dualism that pervades the fundamental form of all sociation."[174] This dualism is "fluctuating, constantly developing life-process that nevertheless also in a relatively stable form."[175]

Ideal types therefore can refer to collectivities such as states and countries; epochs such as the Renaissance; or even cultural or social forms such as economy, exchange, and custom. What an ideal type "must do is to become reducible to the action or probability of action in individuals."[176]

Typifying a rational pattern or law approximated into an adoption or contrivance of an idea is something Plato knew well.

Essentially, Plato's *physis,* the nature of flux and change, is in itself a typified construction of the continuous and cycling being. Plato's ideal typical constructs and contrivances furnish the very standard of an unreality—and yet an explainable rational concept upheld in duties, laws, culture, and customs that begins to describe and ritualize chaotic matter.

To render it into a stance, therefore, or to achieve something so demarcated as a "status," an object standing against us, is rather missing the clouds for the trees. These are constructions, contrivances, and oppositional relationships of an unreality wishing to be upheld in its "pure" thought by social commentators, historians, families, and generations—or dare we say an ethos. Status and stance critiques a *physis* and being, the nature of cosmos and the ebbs and flows of the universe. In other words, to ebb and flow always seems to be glorified in some way, substituted into a new form, and reproduced in every generation, renamed, and reissued.

What now?

Are we back to Passion or Reason?

Activity/Passivity?

8

Passion

Freedom, an interruption of the determinism of war and matter, does not yet escape and takes place in time and history.

—Emmanuel Levinas[177]

As Hélène Cixous goes through her list of oppositional dualisms, the places between activity and passivity, she makes an interesting move. She positions nature as passive. Or does she? Her lists of the oppositional passive feminine qualities lie in a tensional standing with the active masculine positions. There, standing beside Nature, is History—Nature (passive) duels with History (active), then it cycles into Nature/Art, and from there to Nature/Mind. The fourth in these lists of oppositions is rather curious: (1) Nature/History (2) Nature/Art (3) Nature/Mind, and then, oddly (4) Passion/Action.

Why does passion replace nature? Why does passion replace nature in a full extreme category of passivity? Action supposedly has a counterweight in the pendulum—a pure ability to choose, do, think, will, design, or impact. Pure activity expresses historically descending opposition with nature, into art, and into mind—degeneration? Thinking becomes action, but only in its opposition to a purely passive natural form.

Cixous is questioning whether that which shows itself as autonomous really isn't at all. What should be considered activity? Is passion, like nature, purely passive and autonomous at the same time? Is the final opposition, the setting aside of passion, so far removed into a separate categorical nature where action has no ability to freely design, construct, or create? This flips the opposition around, inverts, and makes us ponder.

Passion was once part of a purely active mode, or at least passion was said to be the creative force behind the cosmos. Passion, like Nature, is tactile. Languages turn to activity, from perception to use, from optic to tact. Proximity is therefore important to this story. It has to be felt, and having the unexplainable feeling of its presence is a non-reducible consciousness. Language must constantly interact with a kind of touch given here allegorical of the proximal interplay. The woman, like nature and the natural, is rendered into something indifferent. She is so natural that she is the indifferent cosmic fabric in the backdrop having no effect on us besides the inescapable cyclical ebbs and flows. She is so unnaturally named that she is Gaia, a deification and the fabric of our planetary existence, tools and resources to be actively extracted from. Our linguistic imagery, our dialectical workings, callings, and commanding with the world transfers to each other allegorical to couples, to the substitutional qualities we place upon its ecology. We say nature, we then say passion, and so forth. Our ecological architecture moves from habit to distraction, touch to sight, and back again.[178] The active and passive ebbs and flows teeter-totter from habit to optic, and tactile to habit. Hence if we were to say that we reside in a given ecology, there is a proximal relation felt and indescribable. It can be comparable to architecture of some kind. To Walter Benjamin, even "architecture has never been idle."[179] The natural architecture of our physical reality shows its passions before us as we act with it and say that it does not act nor think. We say that it too must be indifferent, an object standing against us that must be grasped, known, harnessed, and manipulated.

There is something to say of passion as creativity for a moment—as emanation. The passions are either controlled, under maintenance, or enabled. They become our emanating glory that cannot be done away with. A wise man once asked the guru of the gods, Brhaspati, about the greatest of dualisms—good and evil. Brhaspati replied, "All creatures, even gods, are subject to passions. Otherwise the universe, composed as it is of good and evil, could not continue to develop."[180] A powerful ability to harness and control the passions exists. It's equally, if not more, liberating to express them freely.

And what of another way to define action altogether, something found in Nature's passions?

It is *karman* that is our deed, fate, and work. "The end is also found in the means," as Manly P. Hall once said. This is the totality of all work, both good and bad. Inasmuch as *samsara* is an explanatory variable in the scheme of theodicy, the cycle of life-death-life gives a reason for good or bad decisions, and good or bad happenstances.[181] Equally, however, good and evil can be explained away as a problem solved by cycles and ages, just like the primitive conceptions of ages and aeons. The age that characterized man holding a weapon or a pitcher in the night sky, or the rotation is a woman, the cycle is her seasons, or the age of a mankind that was once gold, then silver, then bronze. The rotating stars and signs in the sky are our invariable substitutions. That's a bull; that's a belt; that's another woman. That's time positing to us by the gods. That's a spiritual realm.

Time is a tax, a penance, suffering, or guilt to be given to the next generation as cash flow problems and more replacement values to be reordered. In other words, we are always in a time not perfected; hence, we are suffering; hence, bad things are happening; hence, another name can be given: nature, passion, woman, age, aeon, cycle, era, cosmos, universe, history, gods, so on—a substituted excuse. Proximal relations are felt, indescribable. Words are added and we try to command it.

Passions are held back.

Purely passive.

Passions are harnessed and explained away, substituted by the emanating creativity of the universe itself. Passion becomes the "natural" flow of all things. However, this same creativity and life force is also harnessed as a cycle, as a categorical age, limited by a seasonal interplay of divine, mortal, and universal history. Nature is completely passive, and so is passion, and thus possibly completely active? Active and passive at the same time: there everywhere and never there nowhere or anywhere.

The flux/stability duality—the passion, the appetite, the obsession: unbridled, unthinking, unreflective movement. We say it's autonomous and therefore "natural." Something else is held stable by our substitutions and proximities rendering indifferent and making it stand to us as object by freezing time in our ideally typified thought processes.

We must consider whether all of this is really substitution on a cosmic scale. Must we redefine our "nature" and our "passion" with activities characteristic of substitutional replacement strategies? That makes us wonder if reoccurrence occurs at all. In the spirit of Friedrich Nietzsche, once more we jest at whether these are merely self-deceiving excuses: the unrealities we have idealized, centuries of religious and philosophically ordered concepts and values that are more idol than reality.

Georg Simmel once reflected in sadness about ancient ruins. He considered a cosmic tragedy.

> The collapse strikes us as nature's revenge of the violation which the spirit, by producing a form in its own image, has perpetuated upon it. The balance between nature and spirit, which the building itself presented, shifts in the favor of nature. This shift becomes a cosmic tragedy.[182]

Just covers and cloaks for activity and passivity, it seems?

9
Reconciling, and Dualism

In order for conscious life to be fully self-conscious, it would have to do without concepts altogether, for conceptualization inevitably brings on the reign of forms; yet concepts are essential to self-consciousness. The fact that the possibilities of expression are so limited by the essence of life does not diminish its momentum as an idea.

—Georg Simmel[183]

No need to delve greatly into ancient mysticism. The dialogue *Cratylus* portrayed Socrates playing out a lovely display of etymology and semantics.[184] In it is a wonderful example of dualism inherent in our speech, and how it circulates in interaction with one another. Based on the questions and discussions with his counterpart Hermogenes, Socrates centers on the deity Hermes. Thus the word *hermeneus,* meaning "interpreter," is "a messenger, a thief and a deceiver in words, a wheeler-dealer," and yet all of these descriptions involve speech.[185] Socrates goes forth with derivatives, displaying the word *eirein,* which means to "use words," or from the Homeric tradition it means to "devise or contrive." An extensive etymological examination ensues. Hesiod's *daemons* were named as good men, of honor, destiny, and wisdom who were relational to the next kind of men, *heroes. Heroes,* in turn, are relational to words such as *eros,* "love," sophists as "clever speechmakers" or *rhetores,* and then to "skilled questioners" or *erotan.* From *erotan,* we get the words *eirein* and *legein*[186]—both meaning the same thing which is "to speak."[187] Hermes, the god that devises, is thus calling upon the gods to "contrive speech."[188] Socrates then says: "But we, beautifying the name, as we suppose, call him 'Hermes' nowadays.'"[189]

Socrates then uses a pun. He insults his counterpart Hermogenes, where Cratylus says of Hermogenes that "he is no son of Hermes." As an audience we may be uncertain as to the particularism to which this pun is made, whether it be a literary tool to insult the Hermetic tradition, to revise its definition, or to position a philosophical description, or perhaps all of the above and more. The fascinating thing for us at the moment is that in this pun we observe Socrates at a point of access to the double-nature of speech. In other words, because Hermes is a contriving trickster god, so too is the manifestation of speech. Thus is his double-nature as an all-encompassing, simultaneously everywhere deity: the circulation of language, and a language that can get so complex and varied that it can literally trick us or cover over reality.

The insult continues. Socrates says he agrees that "Hermogenes is no son of Hermes'" since he is "no good at devising speeches" and thus he is more like Pan. [190] Hermogenes thus becomes titled the double-natured son of Hermes because Socrates argues that Hermes has this double-nature in Pan: "You know speech signifies all things (*to pan*) and keeps them circulating and always going about, and that it has two forms"[191] Since Pan is the "all god," and speech must be used to signify all things, it must therefore be circulated everywhere and somehow relate to everything.

Socrates describes the two fold nature of speech; from the upper regions of the gods, it is rather smooth while the rough falsehoods or goatish parts remain among humans. Socrates thus cleverly relates *tragikon* as "goatish" with tragedy of life where "one finds the vast majority of myths and falsehoods."[192]

Here at this moment the important and all-encompassing aspects of speech are defined, while at the same time a transitional "character" begins to perform as if in a tragic "falsehood of myths," or the regalia of ceremonial performance reflected in the "beautification of the gods." Speech doubles and circulates into its lower nature, from contemplation (divine thinking) into activity (acting and mimicry). Socrates concludes his insult and makes a valued distinction between our upper and lower natures:

> Therefore the one who expresses all things (*pan*) and keeps them always in circulation (*aei polōn*) is correctly called 'Pan-the-goat-herd' ('*Pan aipolos*'). The double-natured son of Hermes, he is smooth in his upper parts, and rough and goatish in the ones below. He is either speech itself or the brother of speech, since he is the son of Hermes. And it's not a bit surprising that a brother resembles his brother. But, as I said, let's leave the gods. [193]

In this pun, insult, and clever contriving and devising of philosophical notions by Socrates, we find Hermes and Pan related with each other in that speech circulation is expressed by all that exists in two realms, both equally divine and all-encompassing—the double-nature of our communication with one another. Socrates penetrates these superstitions so abruptly with his etymology that the piety he does relegate to these deities evaporates into a clear notion: There's a doubling phenomenon in our speech. Language and interpretation: The former is derived from an in-depth analysis of "names" or *onoma*. It must be made clear that the Greeks did not have a specific word for "language."[194] The latter, interpretation, is a means by which the name of a deity had to be addressed.

Our upper and lower natures permeate the world, the higher being as the interpretive arts, and the lower as a ubiquitous force, a circulation of everywhere and everyone where the idea of language breaches outside of us autonomously and independently through activity, mimicry, and the perpetuation of myths and falsehoods played out in the tragedies of life. Hans-Georg Gadamer described this phenomenon as the "self-forgetfulness" of language.[195] This explains Aristotle's mysticism also, his divide and in-between features of passion and reason, and of character and practice.

This seems to be the jumping-off point.

Gadamer notes that our linguistic processes are self-forgetting in that they begin to "characterize the performative character of speech."[196] The Greeks were aware of the autonomy that language takes. It happens in a way that is so indiscernible that it simply becomes equated with deity. Even though part of the lower nature, Pan is equated with the ubiquity of language, the performing, the activity, and the dissemination as if herding and being herded everywhere, through all time. It appears to manifest an autonomous life, so indescribable that it must imbue a deified quality. Language and interpretation are also performative in the sense that Pan is goatish and therefore tragic.

Even more curious is the fact that the Greeks did not have a specific word concerning language, at least the way we may wish to consider it. There was a word for "tongue," meaning the sounds that literally emit from the tongue (*glotta*). The notion of *logos* may be applied, although something much more nuanced and complex is happening with this word choice. Gadamer explains:

> With the *logos,* precisely upon which the inner self-forgetfulness of speech is essentially drawn is pushed into view—the world itself which is evoked by speech, lifted into presence, and brought into articulation and communicative participation.[197]

Hence *logos* and *legein* are contrived in a fantastical way as Socrates once mentioned is such an assemblage of our world by speech. Our speech, poetry, song, and sound evoked an indescribability that such a world and reality assemblage had to be part of some higher nature, a divine intercessor deity that could yet contrive and trick us with its complexity at the same time—Hermes.

Resolving dualism, therefore, was once a daunting religious task, even after Socrates, Plato, and Aristotle gave it their own efforts. Later on, for example, Saint Augustine became aware of his earlier heresies that may have resembled these ancient "paganisms." He had to be extra careful while conceptualizing the notion of the "will" positioned between a "carnal" and "spiritual" nature.[198] The Manichean heresy always remained at his doorstep. The omniscient Good and Evil could never be equally paired or coupled. It seems that the assembling and contriving power of speech, and our ubiquitous and interrelated powers with it, are so indescribable that only deifications get close to the mark.

With this perspective and context, it seems odd that moderns would even try to secularize any of this.

But try they did.

Emile Durkheim tried to come to terms with the oppositional binary in a secular fashion by moving the sacred elsewhere altogether. He attempted to resolve it with a new "enlightened" and "scientific" standpoint—the "dualism of human nature."[199] This all-too-modern dualism could be reconciled between the individual and civilization. [200]

Durkheim said dualism in human nature is of course much older. "In every age, man has been intensely aware of this duality."[201] The greatest example can be found in the divide between body and soul. Durkheim contemplates, "There must be something in man that gives rise to this feeling that his nature is dual."[202] Intellectual/Activity, Sensation/Tendency: These are thresholds needing reconciliation through morality.

It begins to divide and double off through conceptual thought and moral activity; both are part of this dual nature in man, something that must be conformed or universalized. Durkheim decides to proceed through morality, something "beginning with disinterest with attachment to something other than ourselves."[203]

Moral activity itself must assume a duality.

There may be no resolution in this doubling nature. "To say that we are double because there are two contrary forces in us is to repeat the problem in different terms—it does not resolve it."[204]

Man has two worlds. "Man is double," says Durkheim, "because two worlds meet in him: that of non intelligent and amoral matter on the one hand, and that of ideas, the spirit, and the good, on the other."[205] An opposition accrues, and thus something becomes "necessary to explain their opposition."[206] Morality is what meets us in these two worlds. Moral activity must assume a duality. Immanuel Kant once said that the individual is conceptually and symbolically sacrificed for duty. Stuck in a paradox of reason, he must strive to be free and yet sacrifice to an obligation to ensure individuality for everyone. Thus conceptual thought and moral activity, once part of this dual nature in man, is also something that must be conformed or universalized. It would make us reluctantly agree that once we try to go further and explain opposition "we understand even less."[207] These "two-worlds" get ever vaguer, and so a living practice alongside our "ethos" is said to be of great importance. Resolution may be found in the space within our thoughts, to enter these paradoxes in the first place, thinking them through and living them out as an experience as a learning development. An ethos assists such matters.

But let's not get ahead of ourselves; the ultimate other outside of our "nature" is still called society, polity, or dare we say a god or universal consciousness of some kind.

Because of "society," groups become the immediate object of any social investigation.[208] It's between individual/group, a dynamic and analysis thereof where the dualism itself becomes the danger. Durkheim spoke eloquently about what was once the separate, dualistic interplay between individual and soul, "the abode of the material world is the abode of the sacred."[209]

The soul must now proceed into new terminology—society and morality. Morality must somehow be reconciled as a dualism because of its discerned detachment; likewise, if morality is invoked, it is an "attachment to something other than ourselves."[210] Durkheim tries to rescue us from this danger with a multiplicity of "concepts." Concepts can commonly become man's plurality because, according to Durkheim, conceptual thought saves us through its active production of plurality that diffuses a heightened and rigid dueling principle. Plurality of man's free interaction with conceptual multiplicity is what can limit, thwart, or at least temper dualisms.

This said, let's look closer at "society," or the brief historical result of Emile Durkheim's societal morality.

Clifford Geertz's critique of "strain theory"[211] provides insight into how conceptual production began with an intention of plurality, something that later is only disguised and screens us from contending with dualisms. Alongside critiques of a historical menu of any and all other ideologies, it makes us wonder.

The Individual/Group dynamic known as "strain" also produces and conceals an invariable amount of potential dualisms. A strain theoretical analysis is an introduction to an extensive amount of newly developed "social categories," something "stabilizing" or "upsetting" the supposed varying "social expectations."[212] Geertz claims that in the end these are merely "individual and group moves" addressed in a newly dualistic mode. As Geertz says, "So also is 'strain,' for it refers both to a state of personal tension and to a condition of social dislocation."[213] What happens is a series of intended conceptual productions becoming "riddled with insoluble antinomies."[214] Reproduced and refreshed dualisms are merely hidden as a functional transitional interplay between notions such as "liberty and political order, stability and change, efficiency and humanity, precision and flexibility, and so forth."[215]

What we call "norms" essentially also play out the duality for us as well. "There are discontinuities between norms in different sectors of society—the economy, the polity, the family and so on."[216] The attempt to set up a theoretical system happens behind the laws of averages and truisms, even an autonomous system still holds the same binary logic of a morality that must be detached or attached likewise.

Something outside of us must exist if only also called a "discrepancy" or "discontinuity," and yet another dualism. Geertz explains, for example, "There are discrepancies between goals with the different sectors—between the emphasis on profit and productivity in business firms or between extending knowledge and disseminating it in universities."[217] What may appear to be a plausible analysis, the gauging of strains, discrepancies, roles, attributes, or newly formed systematic modulations is merely a perpetual duel between stability and strain and thus the repetitive dualistic contentions of our nature. "The clear and distinct idea from which strain theory departs," says Geertz, "is the chronic malintegration of society."[218] Such malintegrated patterns are thus tensional states always necessitating assessments, analysis, and tweaking in design. Or worse, in the political or economic sectors, with the advent and onslaught of "systems," and the mass productions of shouldering and weighing of "concepts" is a power struggle beyond any Machiavellian nightmare.

> The battlefield image of society as a clash of interests thinly disguised as a clash of principles turns attention away from the role that ideologies play in defining (or obscuring) social categories, stabilizing (or upsetting) social expectations, maintain (or undermining) social norms, strengthening (or

weakening) social consensus, relieving (or exacerbating) social tensions.[219]

Thought and its application are the unreality of idols held against the pure idea in a vacuum. Now look at the dualities: Define/Obscure, Stabilize/Upset, Maintain/Undermine, Strength/Weakness, Relieve/Exacerbate—the very tensions and distinctions that are now newly developed multiplicities of binaries to be stuck within, never needing nor wanting resolution, and reproducing these oppositions to reaffirm a theoretical premise and legitimacy of societal governance. Multiple concepts intended to embark on plurality are captured in dualistic binaries that reproduce the old problems of our doubling natures, our two-worlds.

Let's reflect on Durkheim's problem again.

Conceptual Thought/Moral Activity: Hélène Cixous called it the "struggle on two fronts,"[220] what we may interpret as Durkheim's "two-worlds," our thinking self and ego exportation: the individual versus the autonomous collectivity.[221] Even Immanuel Kant's duty has to sacrifice individuality, for "the law of duty cannot be obeyed without humiliating our individual."[222] Thus the obligatory character of society presents itself once more, as overtly, obligatory, and coercively moral[223]

Luce Irigaray[224] once said, however, that the public sphere is the productive realm and authority symbolically held by the man, where the private internalized regions are the feminine. Cixous notes that male privilege is shown not only in the ability to be active versus passive,[225] (one of the greatest dualisms of our time), but in the ability to be inside and outside of the opposition itself; between active and passive; to choose or contain the ability when, where, and how to do so; to have the option to be passive out of preference or active out of convenience. He uses it and he uses this opposition to sustain himself. His action, his choice, and thus a possible privilege is the mere fact that he can not only choose between activity and passivity, but also modulate and choose the opposition itself, build it, construct it, and create it anew. Oppositional frameworks embraced as activity and passivity thereby bring him sustenance.

Something is more indicative of thinking, something primordial. "Thought has always worked through opposition," says Cixous. "A universal battlefield. Each time, a war is let loose."[226] Dual hierarchical oppositions historically produce philosophical orderings of them, and through these "dual hierarchical positions" some kind of "ordering intervenes." In other words, "We see that 'victory' always comes down to the same thing: Things get hierarchical."[227]

Who, where, or what gets to decide and take precedent?

Truth? Fact? Right? Power?

Possession? Opinion? Competition? Obsession?

Cixous puts it plainly: "Organization by hierarchy makes all conceptual organizations subject to man."[228] A privileged choice and potentiality between activity and passivity is a philosophy and ordering of concepts "which gives the appearance of being the condition for the machinery's functioning."[229]

This intervention usually is played out knowingly or in a kind of self-deceit that results in something oppositional. The ordering itself is oppositional in its own right. What resolves? How is it reconciled? Can everyone, everywhere, throughout all time have this privilege, at least in their own thoughts? Could this be possible? Is this not freedom, or at least the first steps into its realm? Thought has to turn into activity. It has to contrive as speech—thinking and doing. We make up new words and substitute with something else.

The game keeps playing along whether you wish to acknowledge it or not.

Produce, substitute, proximate— fatalism?

Acquiescence?

Guilt?

Refresh, negation, refresh, negation, rinse, wash, repeat.

[1] Friedrich Nietzsche, *The Portable Nietzsche,* edited and translated by Walter Kaufmann. (New York: Penguin Books, 1976), 475, in *Twilight of the Idols* Nietzsche spoke of Socrates thusly, "Nor should we forget those auditory hallucinations which as 'the *daimonion* of Socrates,' have been interpreted religiously."

[2] Georg Simmel, *On Individuality and Social Forms,* edited and with and introduction by Donald N. Levine. (Chicago: The University of Chicago Press, 1971), 82, quote modified rarely did Simmel use the word *kampf,* He quite preferred "conflict" to be sociologically described as thus ascertained through an external observation of its striking apart or against something in terms of actual phenomenal visibility—*der streit.*

[3] Ibid., 83

[4] Emmanuel Levinas, *Basic Philosophical Writings,* edited by Adriaan T. Peperzak, Simon Critchley, and Robert Bernasconi. (Bloomington: Indiana University Press, 1996), 99

[5] Ibid., 100

[6] Giorgio Agamben, *The Open: Man and Animal,* translated by Kevin Attell. (Stanford: Stanford University Press, 2004), 10, reliant on Agamben's philosophical interpretation of Alexandre Kojève's *Introduction to the Reading of Hegel*

[7] Emmanuel Levinas, *Basic Philosophical Writings,* 98

[8] Ibid., 98

[9] Hans-Georg Gadamer, *The Beginning of Knowledge,* translated by Rod Coltman. (London: Bloomsbury,2016), 94, quote modified

[10] The ancient contentions we shall delve into later on in the following chapters.

[11] Hans-Georg Gadamer, *The Beginning of Knowledge,* 93, footnote 7, as if knowing and anticipating his contemporary problem, Gadamer decided to also use the foreign word "object,"(*objekt*) and "objectivity" (*objektivität*) as well as his own vernacular *gegenständ*

[12] Hans-Georg Gadamer, *The Beginning of Knowledge,* 94

[13] Ibid., 94

[14] Georg Simmel, *On Individuality and Social Forms,* where in his introductory essay Donald N. Levine discusses various scholarly interpretations of Simmelian

"forms" in regard to culture and personality development. Rudolph Weingartner once described Simmel's "forms" as "proto-culture," p. xv-xvi

[15] Georg Simmel, *On Individuality And Social Forms*, 362

[16] Ibid., 389

[17] Ibid., 84

[18] Ibid., quote modified

[19] Ibid., 80, quote modified

[20] Friedrich Nietzsche, *The Portable Nietzsche*, edited and translated by Walter Kaufmann. (New York: Penguin Books, 1976), 465, quote modified from the preface of *Twilight of the Idols*

[21] Ibid., 465

[22] Ayn Rand, *Philosophy: Who Needs It*, introduction by Leonard Peikoff. (New York: Signet, 1984), 9, quote modified

[23] Friedrich Nietzsche, *The Portable Nietzsche*, 473, from *Twilight of the Idols*, "Maxims and Arrows" 44

[24] This is best described by Jürgen Habermas from *Between Facts and Norms: Contributions to a Discourse Theory of Law and Democracy*, translated by William Rehg. (Cambridge: The MIT Press, 1998), 12-14 Peirce's "ideal assertability" provides the principled foundational premise to Habermas's theory of participation.

[25] Robert R. Williams, *Hegel's Ethics of Recognition*, (University of California Press: Berkeley, 1997), 36-39, where Fichte's thought influences and allows Hegel to contrast with his theory of recognition.

[26] Giorgio Agamben, *Creation and Anarchy: The Work of Art and the Religion of Capitalism*, translated by Adam Kotsko. (Stanford University Press: Stanford, 2019), 56, quote modified

[27] Ibid., 56, quote modified

[28] Aristotle, *The Complete Works of Aristotle: The Revised Oxford Translation, Volume Two*, edited by Jonathan Barnes, (Princeton University Press: Princeton, 1984), 2268, 1419 a25, quote modified

[29] Ibid., 2320, 1450 a16

[30] Ibid., 2320, 1450 a16-18

[31] Ibid., 2321 1450 b9, quote modified

[32] Ibid., 2321 1450 b10

[33] Hannah Arendt, *The Life of the Mind,* (New York, Harcourt, Inc., 1978), 161, footnotes 24 and 25, originally cited on p. 235

[34] Giorgio Agamben, *Creation and Anarchy,* 63

[35] Ibid., 51

[36] Ibid., 55-56, 59-60

[37] Ibid., 59

[38] Giorgio Agamben, *Creation and Anarchy*, 65

[39] Ibid., 61

[40] Ibid., 61

[41] I'm modifying "opinion making" from what was once described as the "claimsmaking" process by Joel Best, *Social Problems,* (New York: W.W. Norton & Company, 2008) and by Donileen Loseke, *Thinking About Social Problems: Second Edition,* (New York: Routledge, 2003), where in my previous writings I've likened this phenomenon to the ancient Socratic and Platonic notions described as "name-givers" exemplified in Plato's dialogues *Cratylus, Timaeus,* and *Critias.*

[42] Georg Simmel, *On Individuality And Social Forms,* edited and with an introduction by Donald N. Levine. (Chicago: The University of Chicago Press, 1971), from the "Introduction" by Donald N. Levine p. xi-xii where it's mentioned that Rudolf Weingartner once described Simmel's philosophy of the "forms" this way. Later on in these writings it will become clear how these little proto-cultural packets can be likened to opinion-making, claimsmaking, or name-giving and thus combine with antagonistic gaming.

[43] Friedrich Nietzsche, *The Portable Nietzsche,* edited and translated by Walter Kaufmann. (New York: Penguin Books, 1976), 475

[44] Ibid., 477, quote modified

[45] Ibid.

[46] Ibid.

[47] Ibid.

[48] Ibid., 476

[49] Ibid., 477

[50] Ibid. quote modified

[51] Ibid, 477

[52] Ibid., quote modified

[53] Ibid., 476, quote modified

[54] Ibid.

[55] Ibid.

[56] At the beginning of *Twilight of the Idols* is a vast and comical list of what Freidrich Nietzsche names as "Maxims and Arrows" that he uses in his own declaration of war against ancient and modern idols.

[57] Giorgio Agamben, *Creation and Anarchy: The Work of Art and the Religion of Capitalism,* translated by Adam Kotsko. (Stanford University Press: Stanford, 2019), 60

[58] Emmanuel Levinas, *Basic Philosophical Writings,* edited by Adriaan T. Peperzak, Simon Critchley, and Robert Bernasconi. (Indianapolis: Indiana University Press, 1996), from the 1968 essay titled "Substitution"

[59] Aristotle, *The Complete Works of Aristotle: The Revised Oxford Translation, Volume Two,* edited by Jonathan Barnes, (Princeton University Press: Princeton, 1984), 2268, 1419 b15

[60] Thus would be my interpretation of Aristotle here made with the assistance of Philip Pettit's *Republicanism: A Theory of Freedom and Government,* (Oxford: Oxford University Press, 1999)

[61] Ibid., 2268, 1419 a10

[62] Ibid., 2268, 1419 a25, quote modified

[63] Ibid., 2154, 1355 a15

[64] Ibid., 2152, 1354 a3

[65] Ibid., 2152, 1354 a16, quote modified

[66] Ibid., 2154, 1355 a26

[67] Ibid., 2152, 1354 a19

[68] Hannah Arendt, *The Life of the Mind,* 62

[69] Ibid., 63

[70] Ibid., 61

[71] Hannah Arendt, *The Life of the Mind,* (New York, Harcourt, Inc., 1978), 216, where Arendt's philosophical interpretation of Cato is paramount to the nuances of spectators, judgment, actors, and opinions—much less politics and publicity.

[72] Sun Tzu, *The Art of War,* unabridged audio book (California: Tantor Media Inc., 2002) quotations from Chapter 3, quote modified. It's equally interesting to leave

a playlist going beginning with this book and then several hours later, on auto-play, are self-help books, business marketing strategies, and how to make money or modulate your cash flow. The "art of war" quite literally turns into a war between you and the economy; the ascertainment of wealth, success, or prestige is the object of warfare.

[73] Michel Foucault, *Ethics: Subjectivity and Truth, Volume One,* edited by Paul Rabinow and translated by Robert Hurley and others. (New York: The New Press, 1997), 61, quote modified

[74] Ibid., 62

[75] Ibid.

[76] Ibid., quote modified

[77] Ibid., 62

[78] Ibid.

[79] Ibid., 62-63, quote modified

[80] Michel Foucault, *"Society Must Be Defended," Lectures at the Collège de France 1975-1976,* edited by Mauro Bertani, Alessandro Fontana, Francois Ewald, and Arnold I. Davidson, translated by David Macey. (New York: Picador, 2003), 52

[81] Ibid., 52

[82] Ibid.

[83] Ibid., 189, quote modified

[84] Ibid., 193

[85] Ibid., quote modified

[86] Friedrich Nietzsche, *The Portable Nietzsche,* edited and translated by Walter Kaufmann. (New York: Penguin Books, 1976), 478

[87] Ibid., 477, quote modified

[88] Ibid., 465-466

[89] Plato, *Plato: Complete Works,* edited by John M. Cooper and D.S. Hutchinson. (Cambridge: Hackett Publishing Company, 1997), 1052, 417b

[90] Irving M. Copi and Carl Cohen, *Introduction to Logic: Twelfth Edition,* (New Jersey: Upper Saddle River, 2005), 291

[91] Ibid., 291

[92] Walter Benjamin, *Reflections,* edited and with an introduction by Peter Demetz, translated by Edmund Jephcott. (New York: Schocken Books, 1978), from the essay "The Destructive Character" p. 301-303, where a "character" in the historical

materialist play epitomizes negation as he sees everywhere and clears space from everywhere.

[93] Rüdiger Bubner, "Habermas's Concept of Critical Theory," translated by Richard Humphrey from *Habermas Critical Debates,* edited by John B. Thompson and David Held including "A Reply to My Critics" by Jürgen Habermas. (Cambridge: The MIT Press, 1982), p. 42-56, where negation is produced in the German aspect of *kritik.*

[94] *The Oxford Dictionary of English Etymology,* edited by C.T. Onions, with the assistance of G.W.S. Friedrichsen and R.W. Burchfield. (Oxford University Press: Oxford, 1966), 929

[95] Werner Hamacher, "Guilt History: Benjamin's Sketch 'Capitalism as Religion,' *Diacritics,* (Fall-Winter: 32.3-4, 2002), 81-106

[96] Ibid., 81

[97] Irving M. Copi and Carl Cohen, *Introduction to Logic,* 664

[98] Giorgio Agamben, *The Open: Man and Animal,* translated by Kevin Attell, (Stanford: Stanford University Press, 2004), 7, quote modified, this of course is derived from Alexandre Kojève's famous *Introduction to the Reading of Hegel*

[99] Ibid., 7

[100] Jaime Malamud-Goti, *Game Without End: State Terror and the Politics of Justice,* foreword by Libbet Crandon-Malamud. (London: University of Oklahoma Press, 1996)

[101] Recall that Max Horkheimer and Theodor Adorno argued in their famous 1947 *Dialectic of the Enlightenment* that Reason and the Enlightenment brought to fruition an expansion of knowledge through vast modes of production whereby fascism, totalitarianism, and even capitalism would become non differential to each other. In other words, in their own ways, all three totally expand through negation.

[102] Jaime Malamud-Goti, *Game Without End,* 76

[103] Ibid., 75

[104] Ibid.

[105] Ibid., 76, footnote 18, p. 207 originally citing Karl Popper's *The Open Society and Its Enemies*

[106] Ibid.

[107] Ibid., 76-77

[108] Ibid., 78

[109] Hannah Arendt, *The Life of the Mind,* (New York, Harcourt, Inc., 1978), 216, again, Arendt's philosophical interpretation of Cato is not lost to the larger picture of her final philosophical developments regarding our faculties of judgment made with one another.

[110] Hélène Cixous, *The Hélène Cixous Reader,* with a preface by Hélène Cixous and foreword by Jacques Derrida, edited by Susan Sellers. (New York: Routledge, 2004), 37, quote modified

[111] Ibid., 37

[112] Ibid., 38

[113] Ibid., from the foreword by Jacques Derrida p. vii-xiii

[114] Emmanuel Levinas, *Basic Philosophical Writings,* edited by Adriaan T. Peperzak, Simon Critchley, and Robert Bernasconi. (Indianapolis: Indiana University Press, 1996), 162, footnote 194

[115] Hélène Cixous, *The Hélène Cixous Reader,* 38

[116] Hannah Arendt, *The Life of the Mind,* (New York, Harcourt, Inc., 1978)

[117] Emanuel Levinas, *Basic Philosophical Writings,* 11, quote modified

[118] Hélène Cixous, *The Hélène Cixous Reader,* 38

[119] Luce Irigaray, *An Ethics of Sexual Difference,* (New York: Cornell University Press, 1993), 100-103

[120] Emmanuel Levinas, *Basic Philosophical Writings,* 81, quote modified

[121] Emmanuel Levinas, *Basic Philosophical Writings,* 80-81

[122] Hannah Arendt, *The Life of the Mind,* 102

[123] Ibid., 102

[124] Walter Benjamin, *Illuminations,* translated by Harry Zohn, edited and with introduction by Hannah Arendt, preface by Leon Wieseltier. (New York: Schocken Books, 2007), 240, quote modified

[125] Ibid., 240

[126] Friedrich Nietzsche, *The Portable Nietzsche,* edited and translated by Walter Kaufmann. (New York: Penguin Books, 1976), 465, quote modified

[127] Hannah Arendt, *The Life of the Mind,* 62

[128] Ibid., 63

[129] Ibid., 61

[130] Giorgio Agamben, *Creation and Anarchy,* 18

[131] Ibid., 19, 62

[132] Ibid., 62

[133] Ibid., 25

[134] Ibid., 24

[135] Hannah Arendt, *The Life of the Mind,* 142-144

[136] Hélène Cixous, *The Hélène Cixous Reader,* 38

[137] Plato, *Plato: Complete Works,* edited by John M. Cooper and D.S. Hutchinson. (Cambridge: Hackett Publishing Company, 1997), 1020. 381e

[138] Giorgio Agamben, *Stasis: Civil War as a Political Paradigm,* translated by Nicholas Heron. Stanford: (Stanford University Press, 2015), 21

[139] Richard H. Wilkinson, *The Complete Gods and Goddesses of Ancient Egypt,* (New York: Thames & Hudson, 2017), 197

[140] Geraldine Pinch, *Egyptian Mythology: A Guide to the Gods, Goddesses, and Traditions of Ancient Egypt,* (Oxford: Oxford University Press, 2002), 192

[141] Ibid., 192

[142] Richard H. Wilkinson, *The Complete Gods and Goddesses of Ancient Egypt,* 197

[143] Geraldine Pinch, *Egyptian Mythology,* 191

[144] Robert Graves, *The Greek Myths: The Complete and Definitive Edition,* (London: Penguin Books, 2011), 283-284

[145] Geraldine Pinch, *Egyptian Mythology,* 193

[146] Richard H. Wilkinson, *The Complete Gods and Goddesses of Ancient Egypt,* 197

[147] Geraldine Pinch, *Egyptian Mythology,* 193

[148] Richard H. Wilkinson, *The Complete Gods and Goddesses of Ancient Egypt,* 197, quote modified

[149] Giorgio Agamben, *Stasis: Civil War as a Political Paradigm,* 8, quote modified

[150] Hans-Georg Gadamer, *The Beginning of Knowledge,* translated by Rod Coltman. London: Bloomsbury, 2016), 94-95

[151] Hans-Georg Gadamer, *The Beginning of Philosophy,* translated by Rod Coltman. London: Bloomsbury, 2016), 52, quote modified

[152] Ibid., 52-53

[153] Ibid., 55, quote modified

[154] Ibid., 6, quote modified, although it must be noted that other English interpretations of this dialogue read quite differently, from Plato, *Plato: Complete Works*, 243e-244a

[155] Hans-Georg Gadamer, *The Beginning of Philosophy*, 15

[156] Ibid., 7

[157] Ibid., 7, once again other English translations vary from Plato, *Plato: Complete Works*, 1098, 471a

[158] Giorgio Agamben, *Stasis: Civil War as a Political Paradigm*, translated by Nicholas Heron. (Stanford: Stanford University Press, 2015)

[159] Ibid., 13-14

[160] Daniel J. Boorstin, *The Creators: A History of Heroes of the Imagination*, (New York: Vintage Books, 1993), 206-207, quote modified

[161] Ibid., 207, quote modified

[162] Ibid., 207

[163] Henry George Liddell and Robert Scott [1909] 2007 *Liddell and Scott's Greek-English Lexicon* Oxford: Simon Wallenberg Press: 647-648

[164] Hans-Georg Gadamer, *The Beginning of Philosophy*, 55

[165] Giorgio Agamben, *Stasis*, 17

[166] Ibid., 17

[167] Ibid., 19

[168] Max Weber, Max *Weber: Selections in Translation*, edited by W.G. Runciman, translated by Eric Matthews. (Cambridge: Cambridge University Press, 2007), 5 terminology original to Georg Jellinek

[169] Max Weber, *Economy and Society: Volume One*, edited by Guenther Roth and Claus Wittich. (Berkeley: University of California Press, 1978), 28, footnote 5

[170] Ibid., 4

[171] Ibid., 28 footnote 5

[172] Kurt H. Wolff, *The Sociology of Georg Simmel*, translated, edited and with an introduction by Kurt H. Wolff. (New York: The Free Press,1964), xxxviii, quote modified

[173] Ibid., xl

[174] Ibid., 385

[175] Ibid. quote modified

[176] Max Weber, *Max Weber: Selections in Translation*, 5

[177] Emmanuel Levinas, *Basic Philosophical Writings*, edited by Adriaan T. Peperzak, Simon Critchley, and Robert Bernasconi. (Indianapolis: Indiana University Press, 1996), from the 1974 essay "Essence and Disinterestedness" p. 114

[178] Walter Benjamin, *Illuminations*, translated by Harry Zohn, edited and with introduction by Hannah Arendt, preface by Leon Wieseltier. (New York: Schocken Books, 2007), 240-241

[179] Ibid., 240

[180] Daniel J. Boorstin, *The Seekers: The Story of a Man's Continuing Quest to Understand His World*, (New York: Vintage Books, 1999), 18

[181] Ibid., 114-115, where Giorgio Agamben also notes the semantic, etymological, and philosophical significance between karman, cause, crime, culpability, and guilt in *Karman: A Brief Treatise on Action, Guilt, and Gesture*, translated by Adam Kotsko (Stanford: Stanford University Press, 2018)

[182] Kurt H. Wolff, *The Sociology of Georg Simmel*, translated, edited and with an introduction by Kurt H. Wolff. (New York: The Free Press,1964), from the "introduction," p. xxxviii, quote modified originally cited on p. 1, footnote 55, where a commentator on Simmel's philosophy also added, "This cosmic tragedy is ultimately also the tragedy of Simmel."

[183] Georg Simmel, *On Individuality and Social Forms*, edited and with and introduction by Donald N. Levine. (Chicago: The University of Chicago Press, 1971), 392, footnote 1, from the 1918 essay "The Conflict in Modern Culture"

[184] Plato, *Plato: Complete Works*, edited by John M. Cooper and D.S. Hutchinson. (Cambridge: Hackett Publishing Company, 1997)

[185] Ibid., 126, 408a

[186] Several centuries later Martin Heidegger will find his famous revision of *logos* in *legein*, defining it as a bringing together or assembling into presence from *Being and Time*. Translated by John Macquarrie and Edward Robinson, foreword by Taylor Carman. New York: Harper Perennial, 2008), 57-59.

Giorgio Agamben interprets *legein* from Heidegger as "to gather together into presence" and rightly connects this notion with Plato and Stoic philosophy concerning the "sayable" from *What is Philosophy?* Translated by Lorenzo Chiesa. (Stanford: Stanford University Press, 2018), 43-45

[187] Ibid., 116-117, 398b-398e

[188] Ibid., 126, 408b

[189] Ibid.

[190] Ibid., 126, 408b

[191] Ibid., 126, 408c

[192] Ibid., 126, 408c

[193] Ibid., 126, 408d

[194] Hans-Georg Gadamer, *The Beginning of Knowledge*, translated by Rod Coltman. (London: Bloomsbury, 2016)

[195] Ibid., 96

[196] Ibid., quote modified

[197] Ibid., 96

[198] Hannah Arendt, *The Life of the Mind: One-volume Edition*, (San Diego: A Harvest Book, 1978), 86-88

[199] Emile Durkheim, *On Morality and Society*, edited and with an introduction by Robert N. Bellah. (Chicago: The University of Chicago Press, 1973), 150

[200] A legacy left to Durkheim by his predecessor, Auguste Comte

[201] Emile Durkheim, *On Morality and Society*, 150

[202] Ibid., 150

[203] Ibid.

[204] Ibid., 157, quote modified

[205] Ibid., quote modified

[206] Ibid.

[207] Ibid.

[208] Ibid., 149

[209] Ibid., 150-151, quote modified

[210] Ibid., 150

[211] A theory developed by Robert K. Merton from *Social Theory and Social Structure: Revised and Enlarged Edition*, (London: The Free Press of Glencoe, 1964), a book heavily based on Durkheim's moral and social principles.

[212] Clifford Geertz, *The Interpretation of Cultures*, (New York: Basic Books, 1973), 202-203

[213] Ibid., 203, quote modified

[214] Ibid.

[215] Ibid.

[216] Ibid.

[217] Ibid.

[218] Ibid.

[219] Ibid., 202-203

[220] Hélène Cixous, *The Hélène Cixous Reader,* with a preface by Hélène Cixous and foreword by Jacques Derrida, edited by Susan Sellers. (New York: Routledge, 2004), 29

[221] Emile Durkheim, *On Morality and Society,* 151

[222] Ibid., 151

[223] Ibid., 162

[224] Luce Irigaray, *An Ethics of Sexual Difference,* (New York: Cornell University Press, 1993). 101-104

[225] Hélène Cixous, *The Hélène Cixous Reader,* 38

[226] Ibid., 38

[227] Ibid., quote modified

[228] Ibid.

[229] Ibid., 39

www.ingramcontent.com/pod-product-compliance
Lightning Source LLC
Chambersburg PA
CBHW070303290526
45791CB00003B/1062